P9-BHZ-433

WHAT PEOPLE ARE SAYING ABOUT OUR BOOKS...

"Should be in the library—and kitchen—of every serious cook."

JIM WOOD—Food & Wine Editor—San Francisco Examiner

"A well-organized and user-friendly tribute to many of the state's finest restaurant chefs."

San Francisco Chronicle

"An attractive guide to the best restaurants and inns, offering recipes from their delectable repertoire of menus."

GAIL RUDDER KENT—Country Inns Magazine

"Outstanding cookbook."

HERITAGE NEWSPAPERS

"Nothing caters to visitors as well as this book does."

TONY TOLLNER—Co-owner, Rio Grill

"It's an answer to what to eat, where to eat—and how to do it yourself."

MONTEREY HERALD

"I dare you to browse through these recipes without being tempted to rush to the kitchen."

PAT GRIFFITH—Chief Washington Bureau, Blade Communications Inc.

Books of the "Secrets" Series

CAPE COD'S COOKING SECRETS

CALIFORNIA WINE COUNTRY COOKING SECRETS

SAN FRANCISCO'S COOKING SECRETS

MONTEREY'S COOKING SECRETS

THE GREAT CALIFORNIA COOKBOOK

SAN FRANCISCO'S
COOKING SECRETS

Starring the best restaurants and inns of San Francisco

by
Kathleen DeVanna Fish

Bon Vivant Press
Monterey, California

All rights reserved. No portion of this book may be reproduced or transmitted in any form or by any means, electronic or mechanical, including photocopying, without permission in writing from the publisher, except for the inclusion of brief quotations in a review.

Library of Congress Cataloguing-in-Publication Data

SAN FRANCISCO'S COOKING SECRETS
Starring the best restaurants and inns of San Francisco

Revised third printing, 1993

Fish, Kathleen DeVanna
93-071071
ISBN 1-883214-00-9
$13.95 softcover
Includes indexes
Autobiography page 287

Copyright 1993 by Kathleen DeVanna Fish

Editorial direction by Fred Hernandez
Cover photography by Robert N. Fish
Pat Hathaway Collection photos, pages 5, 244, 246, 247

Published by Bon Vivant Press
a division of The Marketing Arm
P.O. Box 1994
Monterey, CA 93942

Printed in the United States of America
by Publishers Press

CONTENTS

INTRODUCTION 6
ETHNIC FOOD INDEX OF RESTAURANTS . . . 8
GEOGRAPHIC INDEX OF RESTAURANTS
    AND INNS 9
MAP OF SAN FRANCISCO 10
FAVORITE RESTAURANT RECIPES 11
TRIVIA AND HISTORY 18, 246
GUIDE TO RESTAURANTS 24
GUIDE TO INNS 245
CONVERSION INDEX 282
RECIPE INDEX 283

Construction of the Golden Gate Bridge: A gap in the center section

PASSIONATE DINING IN PARADISE

SAN FRANCISCO IS RICH with scenery, history, amusements, world-renowned food and accommodations. So it's easy to overlook the secret hideaways that make you fall in love with this magical city. Let us guide you to those special restaurants and inns.

Included in this book are 15 unforgettable places to stay—romantic inns with only six guest rooms, historic mansions that continue the tradition of impeccable service, posh hotels that cater to their guests' every need. We carefully chose these inns and hotels because their ambiance is enchanting, the service is first-rate, and you can depend on them for comfort. Prices vary from modest to expensive and are listed for each of the inns and hotels.

THEN THERE IS the incomparable food of San Francisco.

San Franciscans are passionate about dining out. Name your favorite type of food: French, Italian, Mexican, Indian, Japanese, vegetarian, South American, Thai, Chinese, Greek or American. San Francisco has it all. It is truly synonymous with good food and elegant dining.

Scene from a San Francisco boarding house, circa 1906

This early version of the Cliff House lasted from 1864 to 1895

The essence of this book is exquisite food. The restaurants were selected on the basis of their innovative cuisine of consistent quality, matched by a distinctive atmosphere. The combination of aesthetic flair and outstanding cooking is magic. "San Francisco's Secrets" will help you find the grand mix of ethnic tastes that distinguishes San Francisco.

CLOSELY-GUARDED RECIPES comprise the basis of this book. Selections include treasured recipes from the inns. The restaurants go one step further: they provide full menus and their secret recipes. The menus and recipes assembled in this collection have been contributed by some of California's most talented chefs. The format is easy to follow, with preparation times ranging from 15 minutes to three hours.

And to help you get into the spirit of romance and adventure, "San Francisco's Secrets" is sprinkled with highlights of the history, legend and lore of this very romantic city. Plus rare photographs that help you understand how San Francisco evolved.

Discover the secrets. Then you can discover the heart of San Francisco.

Cuisine Index

American

Bix, 24
Campton Place, 30
Fog City Diner, 36
Masons, 42
MacArthur Park, 48
Stars, 54
Victor's 60

California Cuisine

Cafe Majestic, 66
Greens, 72
Silks, 80
Square One, 86

Caribbean

Geva's, 92

Chinese

China Moon Cafe, 98
The Mandarin, 104
Tommy Toy's, 110

French

Act IV, 116
Fleur de Lys, 124
French Room, 130
Sherman House, 136
South Park Cafe, 142

Greek/Middle Eastern

Stoyanof's, 148

Indian

Gaylord India Restaurant, 154

Italian

Ciao, 160
Donatello, 166
Kuleto's Italian Restaurant, 172
La Fiammetta, 178
Prego Ristorante, 184

Japanese

Benkay Restaurant, 190
Yamato Restaurant
  & Sushi Bar, 196

Mediterranean

Splendido's, 202

Mexican

Corona Bar & Grill, 210

Seafood

Aqua, 216
Bentley's Seafood Grill, 224
Hayes Street Grill, 232

South American

Alejandro's, 238

GEOGRAPHIC INDEX

CHINATOWN

Yamato Restaurant
& Sushi Bar, 196

CIVIC CENTER

Act IV—Inn at the Opera, 116
Geva's, 92
Hayes Street Grill, 232
Stars, 55

DOWNTOWN & UNION SQUARE

Benkay Restaurant, 190
Campton Place, 30
China Moon Cafe, 98
Clift Hotel—
   French Room, 130, 254
Corona Bar and Grill, 210
Donatello, 166
Fleur de Lys, 124
Kuleto's, 172
Petite Auberge Inn, 262
Westin St. Francis—
   Victor's, 60, 276

FINANCIAL DISTRICT

Aqua, 216
Bentley's Seafood Grill, 224
Bix, 24
Ciao, 160
MacArthur Park, 48
Silks, 80
Square One, 86
Tommy Toy's, 110

GHIRARDELLI & PIER AREA

Fog City Diner, 36
Gaylord India Restaurant, 154
The Mandarin, 104
Splendido's, 202

THE HAIGHT

Spencer House, 270
Victorian Inn on the Park, 274

THE MARINA

Greens, 72

MISSION DISTRICT

The Inn San Francisco, 258

NOB HILL

Masons, 42,
White Swan Inn, 278

PACIFIC HEIGHTS

La Fiammetta, 178
Prego Ristorante, 184
Cafe Majestic—
   The Majestic, 66, 260
The Queen Anne Hotel, 266
The Sherman House, 268

THE RICHMOND

Alejandro's, 238

SUNSET DISTRICT

Stoyanof's Cafe, 148

WESTERN ADDITION

Alamo Square Inn, 248
Archbishops Mansion Inn, 250

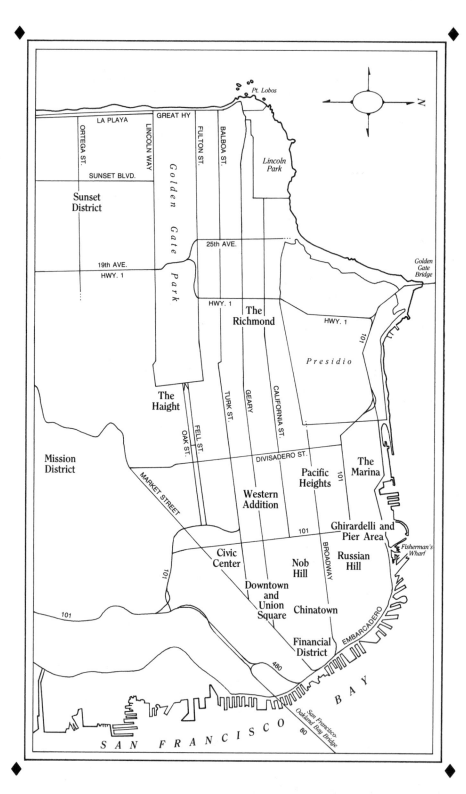

FAVORITE RESTAURANT RECIPES

ACT IV RESTAURANT

Menu for Four   116

RABBIT PIE, GINGER MUSTARD
SWEET ONION MARMALADE
SHERRIED GOLD CHANTERELLES
FILET OF SOLE
MIXED BABY BEETS
SWEET ANISE CORNBREAD
CHOCOLATE VANILLA MOUSSE

AQUA

Menu for Four   217

CARPACCIO OF WILD SALMON
AQUA CRAB CAKES
SAVORY BLACK MUSSEL SOUFFLÉ
WARM TROUT SALAD
CHOCOLATE TORTE

ALEJANDRO'S

Menu for Eight   238

JICAMA SALAD
PRAWN SOUP
CHEESE & JALAPEÑO EGGROLLS
PAELLA
BROWN CUSTARD

BENKAY RESTAURANT

Menu for Four   190

SMOKED SALMON ASPARAGUS
JAPANESE CHICKEN
ROAST DUCK WITH MUSTARD SAUCE
LOBSTER TERIYAKI
CRAB WITH HOLLANDAISE

BENTLEY'S SEAFOOD GRILL

Menu for Eight   224

CRAB CAKES
SEAFOOD SAUSAGE GUMBO
SALMON IN HONEY MUSTARD
PRAWNS WITH RED PEPPER JAM
APPLE & BLUEBERRY TARTLETS

BIX

Menu for Four   24

BIX TARTARE
WALDORF SALAD
DIJON VINAIGRETTE
CHICKEN HASH
CREME BRULÉE

CAFE MAJESTIC

Menu for Six   66

PUMPKIN & PEPPER SLIPPERS
SCALLOP & PRAWN SALAD
RAINBOW VEGETABLE TERRINE
ROAST TURKEY
CORN, CHERRY & RICE STUFFING
MAJESTIC TIRAMISÚ

CAMPTON PLACE

Menu for Six   30

SHIITAKE & OLIVE TAPENADE
ARTICHOKE SOUP
ROAST HEN, ROSEMARY POLENTA
CREME BRULÉE, MINT, BERRIES

CHINA MOON CAFE

Menu for Six   98

SWEET MAMA SQUASH SOUP
FIVE-SPICE DUCK BREASTS
CRUNCHY CABBAGE SLAW
PICKLED GINGER
SPICY GINGER MOONS

CIAO

Menu for Four   160

MARINATED GRILLED RADICCHIO
EGGPLANT & MOZZARELLA
FETTUCCINE, PANCETTA & CREAM
STUFFED CHICKEN BREASTS
VALENTINO

CORONA BAR & GRILL

Menu for Four   210

CEVICHE OF TUNA
SALAD OF FRUIT & CHEESE
HERBED VENISON
TAMALE OF SWEET CORN
PUMPKIN PIE, GUAVA ICE CREAM

DONATELLO

Menu for Six   166

BEET & BEAN SALAD
PASTA PHEASANT RAGOUT
HALIBUT FILETS
STUFFED LAMB LOIN
RISOTTO TAMBALES

FLEUR DE LYS

Menu for Four   124

SALMON IN CORN PANCAKE
CHICKEN, HAZELNUT SAUCE
CREME BRULÉE & APPLES

FOG CITY DINER

Menu for Four   36

GARLIC CUSTARD
SPICY SCALLOPS
ARUGULA PROSCIUTTO SALAD
CHICKEN CURRY POT PIE
POPPYSEED CAKE

FRENCH ROOM

Menu for Four   130

CLAMS WITH SAFFRON
MARINATED ARTICHOKE SALAD
DOLMAS
PORK & EGGPLANT BANDERILLAS
EMPANADILLAS
ORANGE FLAN

GAYLORD INDIA

Menu for Four   154

LENTIL SOUP
LAMB SHAHI KORMA
TANDOORI CHICKEN
RICE PILLAU
KHEER

GEVA'S

Menu for Eight   92

JERK CHICKEN
SHRIMP SALAD
LIME GARLIC SHRIMP
CURRIED GOAT
SWEET POTATO PONE

GREENS

Menu for Six   72

SQUASH & LEEK SOUP
PEAR & WALNUT SALAD
GRILLED VEGETABLES
RAGOUT WITH POLENTA
PLUM ALMOND TART

HAYES STREET GRILL

Menu for Six   232

CLAMS IN BLACK BEAN SAUCE
CALAMARI ARTICHOKE SALAD
SALMON IN BEURRE BLANC
CREME BRULÉE

KULETO'S ITALIAN RESTAURANT

Menu for Four   172

BAKED CHEVRE
FOCCACIA SOUP
MUSHROOM FETTUCCINE
CHICKEN IN PEPPER SAUCE

LA FIAMMETTA

Menu for Four   178

GRILLED RADICCHIO
EGGPLANT SALAD
RISOTTO BIANCO
FILET MIGNON
RASPBERRY WALNUT TART

MACARTHUR PARK

Menu for Four   48

SALAD, CHAMPAGNE VINAIGRETTE
GRILLED PEPPERS
MUSSELS, TOMATO SAFFRON BROTH
SKIRT STEAK, JALAPEÑO JELLY
SWEET POTATO FRIES
CHOCOLATE BLACK WALNUT PIE

THE MANDARIN

Menu for Four   104

HOT & SOUR SOUP
MINCED SQUAB
MONGOLIAN LAMB
RED-COOKED EGGPLANT
GLAZED BANANAS

MASONS

Menu for Six   42

CARIBBEAN CHICKEN
CORN & LOBSTER FRITTERS
LAMB, PINTO BEANS
ROASTED GARLIC
MACADAMIA NUT SOUFFLÉ

PREGO RISTORANTE

Menu for Six   184

SHRIMP & FETA CHEESE
TUNA WITH WHITE BEANS
PASTA, ARTICHOKES, PANCETTA
VEAL IN TOMATO SAUCE

SHERMAN HOUSE

Menu for Four   268

WINTER SQUASH SOUP
CARDAMON BISCUITS
PILLOWS OF LOBSTER
BRAISED RABBIT
FRUITS SABAYON

SILKS

Menu for Six   80

PEAR & SQUASH SOUP
LEMON MISO DRESSING
CORIANDER CURED SALMON
GRILLED CHICKEN
FLOURLESS CHOCOLATE CAKE

SOUTH PARK CAFE

Menu for Eight   142

SALAD D'AVIGNON
BRIE IN PASTRY
SALMON IN FENNEL
RABBIT WITH MUSTARD
LEMON TART

SPLENDIDO'S

Menu for Eight   202

BRESAOLA
RATATOUILLE SALAD
PASTA, CLAMS, WHITE BEANS
PEPPERED TUNA
BEAUJOLAIS GRANITE
BLACK PEPPER BUTTER COOKIES

STAR'S

Menu for Four   54

CREAM OF CORN SOUP
WARM CABBAGE SALAD
BRAISED LAMB SHANKS
GRILLED SQUAB MARINATED
IN BERRY PURÉE
SPONGE CAKE
(RECIPE BY EMILY LUCHETTI)

SQUARE ONE

Menu for Four   86

SMOKED TROUT PATÉ
FATTOUSH
PEA & LETTUCE SOUP
CHICKEN IN FIVE-SPICE
CARAMEL POT DE CREME

STOYANOF'S

Menu for Eight   148

PRAWNS WITH FETA
CUCUMBER DIP
SPANAKOPITA
LEG OF LAMB
TURKISH COOKIES

TOMMY TOY'S

Menu for Four   110

LOBSTER IN MANGO CUP
BLACK MUSHROOMS
CHICKEN, LEMON & CHILES
WON TON CRAB
VANILLA PRAWNS

VICTOR'S

Menu for Four   60

HOT AVOCADO SOUP
SALTED COD ON ONIONS
CRAB SALAD
LAMB EN CROUTE
PANNEQUET OF BERRIES

YAMATO RESTAURANT

Menu for Four   196

SOY BEAN SOUP
EGGPLANT CHICKEN
SEAFOOD VEGETABLE TEMPURA
BEEF & VEGETABLE SUKIYAKI

THE ABUNDANT FEAST

'THE TRUTH IS," wrote historian Joseph Henry Jackson, "San Franciscans have always been sympathetic to the great art of eating and drinking."

The overnight opulence spawned by the Gold Rush prompted an instant demand for places to spend all that new money. Food was abundant in San Francisco because of its proximity to the sea, lush farmlands, ranches and game forests. The diversity of nationalities produced a rich cuisine of tastes and cooking secrets from all over the world.

Restaurants sprang up quickly after the Gold Rush. Marchand's was the place to go for onion soup. The Pup was noted for its fish cooked in wine.

Smaller places spiced the San Francisco food scene with the tastes of many cultures. Quickly absorbed into the cuisine were the spices and methods of the Chinese, Italians, Mexicans, Germans, Spanish, English and Americans.

Lavish Sunday breakfasts were a specialty at the Cliff House, jutting out over the Pacific since the 1860's.

By the 1890's San Francisco was compared with Paris, both for its fine food and for its bawdy morality.

Even after the 1906 quake eateries sprang up quickly

French sauces and soufflés were specialties of three restaurants: the Maison Riche, Maison Doree and the Poodle Dog. An added feature of those lusty restaurants were the private dining rooms above the main restaurant. The private rooms featured couches, private entrances and locks on the doors. It was not rare for female companions to join men friends for a lavish feast and romantic rendezvous.

Other eateries of note included the St. Germaine and the Jules, which were the first restaurants to install slot machines. Their main claim to fame was offering an eight-course dinner and a bottle of wine for 50 cents. But the best bargains were the French family-style restaurants that offered a tureen of soup, salad, a fish course, roasts, vegetables, bread, fruit, coffee, dessert and a glass of wine—all for 25 cents.

Perhaps the best location of the early restaurants was The Castle, whose lofty site atop Telegraph Hill was reached by a special cable car. Its German specialties drew throngs until the place burned down a few years before the 1906 earthquake and fire.

But the queen of all the restaurants was the Palace Hotel, which boasted that it could prepare any dish ordered by its customers, no matter where the dish originated. The opulence of the Palace was a feast for the eyes, and Christmas there was described as a "gastronomic orgy."

Tales abound about the origins of special dishes. They say that the oyster cocktail was invented by a hungry miner while waiting for his dinner. He dumped a few "California raws" into his whiskey and added a dash of catsup, horseradish and Worcestershire. Today's visitors to Fisherman's Wharf can still enjoy a version of the famous walk-away cocktail.

An important addition of the San Francisco food scene was the famed sourdough bread. The long, thin loaves with the unique flavor have been a local delicacy for many years. Sourdough bread led to the creation of the oyster loaf in the 1930's. Fresh fried oysters were cooked to a mouth-watering consistency before being stuffed into the aromatic bread.

BUT MAN DOES NOT live by bread alone. Surrounded by the best wineries in the country and boasting one bar for every 100 inhabitants, San Francisco developed rich cocktail traditions.

It is said that the first cocktail ever made was mixed in San Francisco. The Gold Rush Sazerac contained rye, absinthe, bitters, ice and a touch of anisette. It was the drink of its era.

Another San Francisco original is the Tom and Jerry. It was invented and, in a convoluted manner, was named after its illustrious inventor, Professor Jerry Thomas, who was dubbed America's greatest bartender.

And they say that Irish coffee was first served at the Buena Vista Cafe.

Perhaps the rich San Francisco tradition of fine food and drink is best exemplified by a quick examination of a noted Gay Nineties saloon.

Nichol's Bank Exchange displayed $100,000 worth of art on its walls. The floors were marble, the chandeliers were crystal, and ladies were allowed entry. From 4 p.m. to 11 p.m., it provided a free lunch. It consisted of crab salad, pigs' heads, head cheese, Bolinas Bay clams, beans, chili with meat, sausages, fried clams, sardines, boiled ham, terrapin soup, veal, chicken, corned beef, stewed beef, chipped beef, pork and beans, sliced tongue, smoked salmon, cracked crab, herring, cheese and crackers, popcorn, nuts and fruit. All for the price of a drink.

The tradition of exceptional food continues to the present day. San Francisco remains at the center of innovative cuisine. The recipes in this book will convince you that the abundant feast that began with the Gold Rush has matured to the point that San Francisco is synonymous with fine food.

They used to call San Francisco "The City That Knows How." Perhaps they really meant The City That Knows How to Eat and Drink Well.

SAN FRANCISCO...
HOW IT ALL BEGAN

THERE WAS GOLD—and plenty of it, in California. Between 1850 and 1853, $65 million worth of gold was brought out of the gold-fields each year. Many people got rich as a result of the Gold Rush—and not just by those working the fields. Levi Strauss, who came to San Francisco intending to provide tents, discovered the demand for sturdy pants. He immediately sent back East for more canvas and began designing his Levi's.

Domingo Ghirardelli was also enticed by the fortunes to be made in the goldfields. However, he found it more profitable to sell the 600 pounds of chocolate he brought from Peru.

Then there was Dr. Henry Cogswell, D.D.S., who became one of San Francisco's wealthiest men during the Gold Rush. He made a massive fortune by accommodating the minery's desire for gold-capped front teeth, which were considered symbols of success.

People were drawn to San Francisco by the excitement of being a part of the beginning of a new place. And a few of these characters could be classified eccentric.

Henry Cogswell, a successful real estate developer, was a teetotaler who concluded that people drank liquor because there was an inadequate water supply. He therefore contributed twenty drinking fountains to the city, each with a life-sized bust of himself.

21

Joseph Norton proclaimed himself emperor

James Lick, an altruistic fellow, built a mill where he fed and housed his workers exceptionally well, while he himself lived in a one-room shanty and ate poorly. Lick wore old clothes, carrying a sack through the streets, collecting bones for fertilizer. However, at the same time he gave generously to orphanages and animal shelters. It was James Lick who donated the land for the California Academy of Sciences.

A very memorable chap was Joseph Norton. Norton who made a fortune in grain speculation, tried to corner the rice market. He failed, and when he couldn't meet his financial obligations for the grain he ordered, he suggested instead that he marry the creditor's daughter. He proclaimed himself Norton Emperor of California and Protector of Mexico, so he offered to make her an empress. He was impressive in his aristocratic attire, which consisted of a plumed hat, military uniform and a sword. Norton was also generous with his nonexistent money. He presented a worthless $3.5 million check to the city to build a bridge over the bay by way of Yerba Buena Island. Fifty years later his bridge was built at the cost of $77 million.

Norton's two dogs, Bumer and Lazarus, had the run of the city. When they died, they received a public funeral before being stuffed and presented to the de Young Museum. The dogs, however, are no longer on display.

THE RAPID GROWTH of early San Francisco caused many problems. Ninety percent of the population was composed of male transients who spent much of their time in the 300-plus gambling houses. An area devoted to gambling, drinking and prostitution evolved around the waterfront. There was no established legal system to be enforced by the twelve policemen, who didn't even have a jail.

Ship captains were strongly advised to avoid San Francisco and sail directly to Honolulu, thereby eluding the temptations that awaited their crew.

MONEY AND AFFLUENCE brought an interest in "society." Wealthy San Franciscans spent time giving parties in their extraordinary homes and socializing at the opera or theater. Yachts were chartered for boat excursions on the bay. Culturally, San Francisco began to take itself very seriously.

Overnight, the painted ladies, as the Victorian houses were called, began to transform San Francisco from a boxlike frontier town to a cosmopolitan city. Distinguishable for their jutting bay windows, stained glass and elaborate color combinations, the Victorians were lived in and loved. The Golden Gate became a busy artery for the cargoes of crystal chandeliers and fine furniture from Asia and Europe for these homes.

One of the most successful banks established was the Bank of America, originally called The Bank of Italy in 1849. The founder, Amadeo Peter Giannini, effectively solicited small deposits from people who had not bothered with banks. Giannini's ingenuity worked in his favor during the earthquake. Because he was small, he was able to carry his assets and records to his home outside the city, before the fire came. The day after the quake, a holiday had to be declared to prevent a run on banks because the money lying in the steel vaults was too hot to touch. Of course, Giannini's depositor's funds were available. He also introduced branch banking, which enabled him to pay dividends during a slow economy.

BIX

AMERICAN
56 Gold Street
433-6300
Lunch and dinner Monday–Friday 11:30AM–11:30PM
Saturday 11:30AM–Midnight
6PM–10PM Sunday
Full Bar
AVERAGE DINNER FOR TWO: $50

ENTER THROUGH THE double doors off a quiet alley into an Art Deco setting. Once inside, your attention is drawn to a colorful mural of a jazz club scene above the bar. Reproductions of old ceiling lamps and curving mahogany columns set the mood of a stylish supper club. In the evening, a piano and jazz performance create a 30's atmosphere.

The menu at Bix concentrates on popular classic American dishes with modern culinary touches—the famous Bix's chicken hash or sweet-corn custard, zinfandel braised short ribs, salmon with truffles, soft-shell crabs in garlic butter and desserts like chocolate pecan pie with toffee sauce and bananas foster.

Bix is a place for unhurried dining, listening to some good jazz and going back in time to the 1930's.

Chef Gordon Drysdale's Menu for Four

Bix Tartare
Waldorf Salad with Blue Cheese
Dijon Vinaigrette
Chicken Hash
Creme Brulée

Bix Tartare

Preparation Time: 15 Minutes

1 lb. beef tenderloin
4 egg yolks
6 pieces dark rye bread
4 Tbsps. butter
½ cup cornichons, minced
½ bunch Italian parsley
4 Tbsps. shallots, minced
4 Tbsps. green peppercorns, minced
4 Tbsps. capers, minced
2 Tbsps. anchovies, minced

Completely clear beef of all fat and silver skin. Dice into ½" pieces. Chop in processor.

Mound the beef into a patty and place in the center of the plate. Capture the yolks, in half of the shell, and press into the center of the patty.

Toast bread, de-crust and spread with butter. Cut in half and arrange around half of the plate. On the other half of the plate arrange remaining ingredients in individual piles.

Waldorf Salad with Blue Cheese

Preparation Time: 15 Minutes

1 cup butter lettuce	1 cup walnuts
1 cup chicory	1 celery stalk, minced
1 cup arugula	½ cup mayonnaise
¾ cup Dijon vinaigrette	½ bunch parsley, minced
4 Granny Smith apples	½ cup Roquefort cheese, crumbled

Combine the greens and dress with half the Dijon vinaigrette. Arrange on a plate.

Combine apples, walnuts and celery. Dress with Dijon vinaigrette and place on bed of greens in the center. Top with a dollop of mayonnaise and sprinkle with parsley and Roquefort crumbles.

Cooking tip: Do not overdress the greens or apple celery mixture.

Dijon Vinaigrette

Preparation Time: 10 Minutes
Yield: 1 Quart

½ cup Dijon mustard
1 cup champagne vinegar
4 Tbsps. shallots
1½ tsps. sea salt
¾ tsp. white pepper
3 cups olive oil

Blend the mustard, vinegar, shallots, salt and pepper slowly in a large bowl. Whisk in the olive oil, until emulsified.

Serve at room temperature. Refrigerate between uses.

Bix's Chicken Hash with Grits

Preparation Time: 1½ Hours
Pre-heat oven to 400°

Grits

One 3 lb. chicken
1 cup carrots, chopped
1 cup celery, chopped
1 cup onions, chopped
1 bay leaf
3 black peppercorns
3 ears corn, grated
½ tsp. garlic, minced
1 Tbsp. shallots
½ tsp. butter
¼ cup white corn grits
¼ cup cream
Salt and pepper to taste

In a large pot, cover the chicken with cold water and flavor with carrots, celery, onion, bay leaf and peppercorns. Bring to a boil over high heat. Remove from heat and let sit submerged for 50 minutes.

Remove chicken from water and cool. Remove meat and dice. Save the stock for sauce.

Prepare the grits by grating the corn on a box grater, reserving all the liquids.

Sauté the garlic and shallots in butter until color begins to turn. Add grated corn and stir. Add grits and cream. Bake at 400° for about 10–15 minutes, stirring occasionally.

When the grits are dry, remove to a tray and cool. Season with salt and pepper.

Bix's Chicken Hash

2 ears corn
½ bunch scallions, diced
¼ red onion, diced
1 egg
¼ cup flour
   Salt and pepper to taste
   Olive oil for sautéing

Cut kernels off the corn cobs and place in a large bowl. Add scallions, the reserved chicken, onions, egg and flour. Mix thoroughly, season with salt and pepper.

Heat a little olive oil in a non-stick pan. When oil is smoking, slide hash into the pan and brown on one side.

Finish in a 400° oven for 5–6 minutes.

Serve hot on top of warm sauce.

Sauce

½ tsp. garlic, minced   **Reserved stock**
1 tsp. shallots, minced   **1 Tbsp. basil, minced**
1 Tbsp. tomato paste   **1 Tbsp. parsley, chopped**
  Splash of white wine   **Salt and pepper to taste**
  Splash of champagne vinegar **4 oz. butter, cold**
4 whole tomatoes, diced,
   no skins or seeds

Sauté the garlic and shallots in a tsp. of butter, until golden in color. Add the tomato paste and toss. Mix in the wine and vinegar. Add the tomatoes, stock, basil and parsley. Season with salt and pepper and let simmer until thick, 1 to 2 minutes. Add remaining butter and let sauce reduce to a thick consistency.

Bix Creme Brulée

Preparation Time: One hour
Pre-heat oven to 350°

   1 qt. heavy cream
   1 vanilla bean, split and scraped
   ½ cup sugar
   6 large egg yolks

   Bring the cream and vanilla bean to a simmer. Steep for 10 to 15 minutes.

   Beat the sugar and egg yolks until thick and light in color. Slowly add the cream to the yolks, whisking constantly.

   Pour into 4 oz. custard molds and bake in a shallow waterbath covered with foil for 30 to 40 minutes at 350°, until the custard is smooth, glossy and set.

   Chill and serve as is for a pot-de-creme or sprinkle the top with 1 heaping teaspoon of sugar and caramelize with a baker's iron.

CAMPTON PLACE RESTAURANT

AMERICAN
CAMPTON PLACE HOTEL
340 Stockton Street
781-5555
Monday—Friday 7AM—10PM
Saturday, Sunday 8AM—2:30PM
AVERAGE DINNER FOR TWO: $80—$100

THE RESTAURANT AT Campton Place continues to earn extraordinary acclaim. Here, guests enjoy superb cuisine, fine French and American wines and an ambiance graced by Wedgewood, crystal and cut flowers. Both the menu and wine list are changed frequently. An adjoining 20-seat bar provides a cozy setting for afternoon tea or a rendezvous with friends for cocktails.

Executive chef Jan Birnbaum came to San Francisco with expertise he refined at three well-know kitchens: K-Paul's in New Orleans, the Quilted Giraffe in New York, and the Rattlesnake Dinner Club in Denver. Birnbaum belongs to the new generation of American chefs, having developed a cooking voice of his own and bringing exciting new ideas to create innovative American cuisine.

CAMPTON
PLACE

Executive Chef Jan Birnbaum's Menu for Six

Shiitake Mushrooms with Olive Tapenade
Artichoke Soup
Roast Guinea Hen with Rosemary Polenta & Chanterelles
Creme Brulée with Mint & Berries

Shiitake Mushrooms with Olive Tapenade

Preparation Time: 30 Minutes
Pre-heat oven to 375°

12–18 Shiitake caps, 2–3"
    diameter
2 tsps. rosemary
½ bunch thyme, fresh
¼ cup plus 1 tsp. virgin
    olive oil
10 capers, drained,
    chopped
6 black cured olives,
    pitted, chopped

6 green-brined olives,
    pitted, chopped
1 small shallot, diced
1 Tbsp. Italian parsley,
    chopped
18 long chives
Salt and pepper to taste

Trim mushrooms off at the stem, being sure to cut the stem completely smooth at the cap. Discard the stem.

Combine rosemary, thyme, salt, pepper and olive oil and sprinkle over the mushroom caps. Roast caps at 375° for about 15 minutes. Cool and reserve.

To make the tapenade, combine the capers, black and green olives, shallots and parsley. Season with salt and pepper and toss with virgin olive oil.

To assemble, place roasted mushroom caps on work surface, ribs up. Place a Tbsp. of tapenade in each cap. Fold cap in half and tie into a neat package with the long chives. Place on a serving platter with herb garnishes.

Artichoke Soup

Preparation Time: 2 Hours

8–10 large artichokes
  1 gallon water
  6 lemons
  ¼ cup olive oil
  2 yellow onions, sliced
  8 cloves garlic, chopped coarse
  3 tomatoes, halved
  3 qts. chicken stock
  ¼ bunch fresh thyme
1½ cups cream
    Tabasco to taste
    Salt and pepper to taste

Trim tops and tough outer leaves from artichokes and discard. Peel artichokes almost down to the hearts. Cut artichokes into quarters and reserve in water. Squeeze the juice of the lemons into the water.

In a large pot, sauté onions in olive oil until they begin to brown. Add garlic and sauté 1 to 2 minutes. Place the rest of the ingredients into the pot, except for the cream. Simmer for 1½ hours until the artichokes are soft.

Pass the soup through large holes of a sieve. Return the soup to a boil and add the cream, seasoning with salt and pepper.

Roast Guinea Hen with Rosemary Polenta & Chanterelles

Preparation Time 1½ Hours

      3 guinea hens (chicken can be substituted)
      4 Tbsps. lemon juice
   ¾ lb. butter, soft
      1 cup pine nuts, toasted
      3 Tbsps. Italian parsley, chopped
      2 tsps. sage, chopped
      2 lbs. Chanterelle mushrooms (or any wild mushroom)
      1 basket pearl onions
18–20 baby carrots, peeled
      1 Tbsp. fresh thyme, chopped
        Salt and pepper to taste

In a food processor place the lemon juice, butter, salt and pepper and blend until completely mixed. Add toasted nuts, parsley and sage. In plastic wrap, roll the ingredients into a log, 1½ inches in diameter, and refrigerate. The compound butter can be made up to 3 days ahead, and can be frozen longer.

Allow birds to come to room temperature. Use all the compound butter, except 3″ of the log. Save the rest of compound butter for the polenta sauce. Slice the butter into discs and slide them under the skin of the birds.

If you are going to roast the birds whole, season with seasoning mixture and roast at 375° for about 40 minutes. If birds are halved or boned, sear the skin in a little olive oil and roast under same directions for 15–20 minutes.

About ¾ of the way into roasting the birds, add the pearl onions and carrots to the roasting pan. In the last 10 minutes of roasting, add the Chanterelles and the thyme.

Rosemary Polenta and Sauce

2 cups half & half cream
2 oz. butter
1½ cups water
2½ tsps. fresh rosemary, chopped
¾ cups polenta, coarse ground corn meal
   Salt and pepper to taste

Sauce

1 pt. white wine
1 pt. chicken stock or water
½ cup reserved compound butter

While birds are roasting, bring the cream, butter, water, salt and pepper to a boil with the rosemary. Add corn meal while whisking. Reduce heat, cover and simmer, stirring often. Polenta is ready when graininess is gone.

Remove birds and vegetables from roasting pan, cover and set aside. Drain excess fat from pan. Over medium heat on top of stove, deglaze with white wine, reduce and add stock.

Before serving, bring sauce to a boil and whisk in reserved compound butter.

Cooking tip: This meal is best served family style.

Creme Brulée with Mint & Berries

Preparation Time: 30 Minutes (note refrigeration time)

1 **basket raspberries**
3 **cups heavy cream**
10 **leaves fresh mint**
8 **egg yolks**
4 **Tbsps. sugar**
1 **vanilla bean**
2 **Tbsps. extra fine sugar**

Place 5–6 berries in 6 bowls or custard cups. Set aside.

In heavy sauce pot, bring cream to a boil and simmer for 3 minutes. Remove from heat. Add mint and steep 15 minutes. Strain and reserve.

In a large bowl, whip yolks with sugar until pale yellow, about 5–10 minutes. Add ¼ cup hot cream to yolks while whisking. Continue until cream and yolks are blended.

Over medium heat cook the mixture to a custard texture, stirring and scraping the sides with a flat wooden spoon.

Gently pour the custard into bowls over berries. Chill overnight.

To Brulee (burnt caramel crust) sprinkle the top lightly with extra fine sugar. Preheat the broiler to 550°, placing bowls as close to the flame as possible until the sugar caramelizes.

Fog City Diner

AMERICAN
1300 Battery Street
982-2000
Lunch and dinner served daily 11:30AM–11:30PM
AVERAGE DINNER FOR TWO: $45

THE ULTIMATE 90'S diner. Flashy neon and chrome accented with marble mirrors, mahogany and fantastic food that's fun to eat. You have arrived at Fog City Diner!

Inside the diner is an authentic eight-seat counter, black leather booths with frosted glass booth dividers and an oyster bar. Classic music from the juke box sets the mood of a 30's atmosphere.

Creative American food is cleverly presented. The current menu offers sandwiches such as reddened snapper with guacamole or the 90's version of the chili dog, smothered in chili made from sirloin steak, lamb and pork tenderloin. Various fresh fish and shellfish are always available as well as grilled skirt steak with tomato aioli, grilled sausage and polenta with herbed tomatoes and crabcakes with sherry-cayenne mayonnaise. The large selection of fresh salads, soups and homemade breads are exquisite. Don't forget the American desserts such as root beer floats, milk shakes and malteds and, of course, chocolate brownies with ice cream.

Chef Cindy Pawlcyn's Menu for Four

Garlic Custard with Mushroom Sauce
Spicy Fried Scallops with Ancho Mayonnaise
Arugula, Prosciutto and Pear Salad
Chicken Curry Pot Pie
Poppyseed Cake

Garlic Custard with Mushroom Sauce

Preparation Time: One hour
Pre-heat oven to 270°

1 pt. whipping cream
12 garlic cloves
4 egg yolks
   Freshly ground
   nutmeg to taste
Sweet butter for
   the baking cups
8 large fresh shiitake
   mushrooms, sliced
8 other wild
   mushrooms, sliced

3 whole scallions,
   minced
1 Tbsp. sweet butter,
   plus butter for
   sautéing
2 cups chicken stock
   Salt and white pepper
   to taste
3 Tbsps. chives, minced
⅔ cups walnuts, toasted

To make the custard, slowly simmer the whipping cream and garlic until the cream is reduced by one-third and the garlic is soft. Run this through a food mill and stir in the egg yolks, nutmeg, salt and pepper. Mix thoroughly.

Butter eight two-ounce ramekins or soufflé or custard cups and fill with the custard mixture. Cover the ramekins with buttered parchment and bake in a water bath for 40 minutes at 270°.

Meanwhile, make the sauce. Sauté the mushrooms and scallions in enough butter to coat the bottom of a skillet. When soft, add chicken stock. Over high heat, reduce the liquid by one-third and season with salt and pepper. Turn off the heat.

When the custard is done, turn it out onto the center of a small plate. Reheat the mushroom sauce, stir in one tablespoon of soft butter, add the chives and walnuts and spoon around the garlic custard.

Spicy Fried Scallops with Ancho Mayonnaise

Preparation Time: 45 Minutes

- 13 ½ oz. Maine sea scallops, large
- 1 cup corn meal
- 1 tsp. cayenne
- 1 Tbsp. paprika
- 1 Tbsp. cumin
- 1 Tbsp. salt
- 1 Tbsp. white pepper
- 3 Tbsps. chili powder
- 1 cup homemade mayonnaise
- 3 Tbsps. ancho chili paste
- Ice water
- 1 scallion, minced
- ¼ cup red cabbage, minced
- Lemon wedges for garnish

Combine the corn meal, cayenne, paprika, cumin, salt, pepper and chili powder together.

Dust the scallops with the spice mixture and deep fry at 375° until cooked.

Make the ancho chili mayonnaise by combining the mayonnaise, ancho chili paste and drizzling enough ice water to create a consistency like a heavy cream.

Lay the scallops across the base of a small oval plate. Drizzle with ancho chili mayonnaise. Sprinkle with minced scallions and minced red cabbage. Garnish with lemon wedge.

Cooking tip: The spicy coating is nice on all types of white fish.

Arugula, Prosciutto and Pear Salad

Preparation Time: 15 Minutes

½ cup sherry vinegar
¼ cup honey
2 Tbsps. rosemary, chopped
4 Tbsps. shallots, minced
3 cups olive oil
  Salt and pepper to taste
1½ cups arugula
¼ lb. prosciutto, thinly sliced
1 pear, thinly sliced

In a medium-sized saucepan combine vinegar, honey, rosemary and shallots until warm. Remove from heat and let cool.

Whisk in the olive oil and season the vinaigrette dressing with salt and pepper.

Arrange the prosciutto around the outside edges of the plate. Dress the arugula and pear slices in center with the vinaigrette.

Chicken Curry Pot Pie

Preparation Time: One hour
Pre-heat oven to 350°

  3 **Tbsps. butter**
  ½ **cup carrots, julienned**
  ½ **cup corn kernels**
  ¾ **cup crimini mushrooms, sliced**
  ½ **cup peas**
  1 **medium potato, cooked, diced**
     Pinch of salt and pepper
1½ **cups chicken, cooked, diced**
  ½ **cup chicken stock**
  2 **Tbsps. veloute* (heaping)**
  1 **tsp. curry powder**
  ½ **cup cream**
  2 **tsps. parsley, minced**
     Pie crust for topping
     Egg wash (mix 1 egg and 1 Tbsp. water)

Sauté carrots, corn and mushrooms in 2 Tbsps. butter for 3 minutes. Add peas and potatoes, cooking for 1 minute more. Season with salt and pepper. Add chicken and deglaze with stock. Whisk in veloute and let simmer. Add remaining ingredients. Reduce by one third. Finish with 1 Tbsp. butter.

Pour into a soufflé dish and top with your favorite pie crust. Egg-wash and bake until golden, approximately 25 minutes.

*Veloute is a rich white sauce made from meat stock thickened with flour and butter.

Poppyseed Cake

Preparation Time: One hour (note soaking time)
Pre-heat oven to 350°

  2 oz. poppyseeds
  1 cup buttermilk
  1 cup butter
1½ cups sugar
  4 eggs
  1 tsp. almond extract
2½ cups flour
  1 tsp. baking soda
  2 tsps. baking powder
  ½ tsp. salt
  2 Tbsps. zest of lemon, finely grated

Soak poppyseeds in buttermilk one hour before baking.

Cream the butter and 1 cup sugar until light and creamy. Add 4 egg yolks and almond extract. Beat well and set aside.

In a large bowl sift the flour, baking soda, baking powder and salt. Add the egg mixture, poppyseeds, buttermilk and zest of lemon.

In a separate bowl beat 4 egg whites with ½ cup sugar until stiff but not dry. Fold the egg whites into the flour mixture.

Pour into a buttered and floured pan. Bake at 350° for 45 minutes.

MASONS RESTAURANT

AMERICAN
FAIRMONT HOTEL
980 California Street
392-0113
Dinner Monday–Saturday from 6PM
AVERAGE DINNER FOR TWO: $80

CLASSIC AMERICAN CUISINE accentuated with popular sauces, herbs and spices describes the dishes served here.

Masons is located in the legendary Fairmont Hotel atop Nob Hill, offering panoramic views. One of San Francisco's most beautiful and romantic restaurants, Masons combines highly elegant decor with a warm and relaxed atmosphere. The restaurant has a quiet, club appeal, where guests nestle into intimate banquettes.

One of Masons' unique features is the kiawe (pronounced "key-ah' vee") grill. Named for the special Hawaiian wood used, Kiawe imparts a delicate, tantalizing flavor to meats and fish on Masons' well-rounded grill menu.

Executive Chef Claude Bougard's Menu for Six

Caribbean Chicken & Spinach Soup
Corn & Lobster Fritters with Nantua Sauce
Braised Lamb Shanks with Pinto Beans,
Roasted Garlic and Creme Fraiche
Macadamia Nut Soufflé

Caribbean Chicken and Spinach Soup

Preparation Time: 2 Hours

3 qts. chicken stock or broth
1 green bell pepper, chopped
1 large onion, chopped
1 carrot, chopped
1 bunch cilantro, chopped (2 cups)
2 celery stalks, chopped
1 Tbsp. whole black pepper
½ Jalapeño pepper, seeds removed
    Milk from 1 coconut (or 3 Tbsps. Coco Lopez)
¼ cup dry polenta (cornmeal)
3 half chicken breasts cut into ¼" thick strips
2 bunches spinach, washed and julienned (2 cups)
    Shredded coconut for garnish

Put the first 9 ingredients in a saucepan, bring to a boil. Lower the heat and simmer for 1½ hours.

Strain out the vegetables and return to low heat. Add the polenta and simmer for 20 minutes.

Add the chicken and continue simmering for 5–10 minutes.

Add the spinach at last minute before serving. Garnish with coconut.

Corn and Lobster Fritters with Nantua Sauce

Preparation Time: 3 Hours

Nantua Sauce

Two 1¼ lb. lobsters
3 Tbsps. olive oil
2 stalks celery, chopped
2 carrots, chopped
1 large onion, chopped
½ cup brandy
2 Tbsps. tomato paste
1 bunch parsley (2 cups)
1 tsp. thyme leaf
3 bay leaves
1 gallon water
1 cup cream

Boil the lobsters for 3 minutes. Remove claw and tail meat and refrigerate. Crush shells and bodies with cleaver to simmer in sauce.

Heat the oil in a large saucepan until hot. Add all the vegetables and crushed lobster. Stir frequently until the vegetables are tender. Deglaze with brandy. Add the tomato paste, herbs and water, then bring the sauce to a boil. Lower the heat and simmer for 2½ to 3 hours.

Strain liquid into another heavy saucepan and bring to a boil, reducing to 2 cups. Add cream and reduce again to 2 cups. Keep warm until ready to use.

Fritter Batter

Vegetable oil for frying
5 eggs
2 Tbsps. masa harina flour
1 Tbsp. flour
1 tsp. salt
¼ tsp. baking powder
1 ear fresh corn, uncooked, kernels removed
Chive and roasted pepper garnish

Place vegetable oil into large sauté pan, to yield liquid 1-inch deep.

Separate the egg whites and yolk, beating the egg yolks, until thick and lemony yellow. Add both flours, salt and baking powder. Stir in corn.

In a separate bowl, beat the egg whites until stiff but not dry. Carefully fold the yolk mixture and whites together.

Portion chilled lobster so you get 8–10 pieces. Dredge in flour and dip into fritter batter. Sauté in hot oil, turning 2 to 3 times. Drain on paper towels.

To serve, spoon ¼ cup warmed nantua sauce on each plate, placing lobster fritter in the center of the plate. Garnish with chives and roasted pepper.

Cooking tip: Fritters can be made ahead of time and reheated in 400° oven.

Braised Lamb Shanks with Pinto Beans

Preparation Time: 2 Hours (note pinto bean cooking time)
Pre-heat oven to 450°

  1 lb. pinto beans, washed
½ cup onion, diced
    Small clove of garlic
  6 lamb shanks
¼ cups carrots, diced
¼ cup celery, diced
¼ cup mushrooms, diced
  1 cup red wine
  2 cups veal stock
  1 small sprig fresh rosemary
1–2 bay leaves
  1 large tomato, peeled, seeded and coarsely diced
    Salt and black pepper to taste
½ cup cream
½ cup sour cream

Place pinto beans, ¼ cup onion and garlic in stock pot and cover with 10 inches of water, cooking over low flame for minimum of 4 hours.

Brown shanks in oil. Add carrots, celery, mushrooms and ¼ cup onion. Deglaze with wine and stock. Add herbs and tomatoes. Season with salt and pepper. Bring to a boil, cover and cook for 1 hour and 45 minutes in 450° oven.

To make creme fraiche, blend cream and sour cream together. Store in warm place for 24 hours. Refrigerate.

Serve on a bed of pinto beans. Garnish with creme fraiche.

Macadamia Nut Soufflé

Preparation Time: 15 Minutes (note refrigeration time)

½ lb. sugar
5½ oz. egg whites (5–6 large eggs)
½ quart cream
2½ oz. Amaretto liqueur
½ cup macadamia nuts, toasted and chopped

Over medium heat, cook sugar with enough water to cover, until it forms a soft ball.

Whip the egg whites until they are fluffy, while slowly adding the sugar. Whip for 10 minutes or until the mixture is room temperature.

Whip the cream until light. Fold the cream into the egg whites and add the liqueur and toasted nuts.

Divide into soufflé cups and freeze.

MacArthur Park

AMERICAN
607 Front Street
398-5700
781-5560 Take out
296-7208 FAX Take-out

Lunch Monday–Friday 11:30AM–2:30PM
Dinner Monday–Thursday 5PM–10:30PM
Dinner Friday–Saturday 5PM–11PM
Dinner Sunday 4:30PM–10PM
Continuous bar service
AVERAGE DINNER FOR TWO: $30

VOTED AS HAVING the best barbecue in the Bay Area, Mac-Arthur Park is a restaurant confident in creating delicious food of consistent high quality, like oakwood smoked baby back ribs and chicken, mesquite charcoal-grilled fresh fish and lobster and big steaks. The American wine list is as extensive as the menu, offering many of California's best selections by the glass.

Most foods can be boxed "to go" by calling or faxing your order to the take-out counter. The atmosphere is fun and casual, in a setting of brick walls, polished wood floors, brass railings, skylights and oversized indoor trees.

Great food in a friendly atmosphere at a modest price. That's hard to beat!

Chef Dennis McCarthy's Menu for Four

Mixed Salad with Champagne Vinaigrette
Grilled Pasilla Peppers Filled with Three Cheeses
Steamed Mussels in Tomato and Saffron Broth
Grilled Skirt Steak with Jalapeño Jelly
Sweet Potato Fries
Chocolate Black Walnut Pie

Mixed Baby Lettuce Salad with Champagne Vinaigrette

Preparation Time: 20 Minutes

1 cup champagne vinegar
1 cup orange juice
2 Tbsps. whole grain mustard
1 clove garlic, crushed
1 tsp. salt
1 tsp. cracked black pepper
2½ cups virgin olive oil
4 portions of a mixture of your favorite baby lettuces
2 cups jicama, peeled and cut into thin sticks
1 cup pine nuts, roasted

Blend vinegar, orange juice, mustard, garlic, salt and pepper in a bowl. Slowly add the olive oil and mix until vinaigrette is well blended.

Toss baby lettuces with vinaigrette. Serve topped with jicama sticks and pine nuts.

Grilled Pasilla Peppers Filled with Three Cheeses

Preparation Time: 20 Minutes

    8 large fresh pasilla peppers (2 per person)
    ½ lb. jack cheese, shredded
    ½ lb. cheddar cheese, shredded
    ½ lb. blue cheese, crumbled
    3 Tbsps. olive oil
        Juice of 1½ lemons

Cut off top of pepper and remove seeds and ribs, reserving top. Blanch peppers in boiling water for 1½ minutes. Remove from water and place in an ice water bath, then drain. Mix three cheeses with olive oil and lemon juice. Stuff peppers with the three cheese mixture. Replace top of pepper and grill over coals or broil until skin on outside of pepper is slightly blackened and the cheese inside is melted.

Serve peppers with Salsa Fresca.

Salsa Fresca

    1 ripe tomato, coarsely chopped
    2 jalapeño peppers, coarsely chopped
    1 small red onion, coarsely chopped
    ⅓ bunch cilantro, finely chopped
        Juice of ½ lime
        Salt and black pepper to taste

To make the Salsa Fresca, thoroughly mix together all the ingredients.

Steamed Mussels in Tomato Saffron Broth

Preparation Time: 30 Minutes

1 lb. sweet butter, softened
2 Tbsps. tomato paste
1 pinch saffron, soaked in
   ¼ cup water for 10
   minutes
2 cloves garlic, minced
1 small jalapeño, seeded
   and chopped

1 tsp. parsley, chopped
1 tsp. cilantro, chopped
1 tsp. marjoram, chopped
1 tsp. basil, chopped
1 tsp. chives, chopped
   Juice of one lemon
   Salt and pepper to taste

Combine all ingredients in medium-sized bowl to make tomato and saffron butter. Mix thoroughly and refrigerate.

Broth

2 lbs. black mussels
4 oz. compound butter
2 lemons, cut in half
1½ cups water
1½ cups white wine
1 large tomato, coarsely diced
4 Tbsps. red onion, diced
Parsley for garnish, chopped

Place broth ingredients, except for parsley, in a heavy saucepan. Add tomato and saffron compound butter. Cover and cook over high heat for 4 minutes or until mussels open. Discard any mussels that fail to open.

Spoon mussels into bowls and cover with broth. Sprinkle with parsley and serve immediately.

Grilled Skirt Steak with Jalapeño Jelly & Sweet Potato Fries

Preparation time: 20 Minutes (note marinating time)

2 cups red onion puree
2 cups sweet whole grain
   mustard
½ cup lemon juice

1 cup fresh marjoram,
   chopped
1 cup olive oil
2½ lbs. skirt steak

Combine the first 5 ingredients and mix well. Trim the skirt steak and marinate for 24 hours in the refrigerator. Wipe off excess marinade and grill to desired degree of doneness.

Sweet Potato Fries

1 white sweet potato (yams don't work)
Oil for deep frying
1 bunch large green onions, chopped
1 cup beef consomme (beef stock can substitute)

Cut sweet potato to shoestring size and deep fry in oil until crisp and lightly browned. Drain well. Sauté the green onion in the beef consomme and reserve. Serve steak topped with green onions and jalapeño jelly, with sweet potato fries on the side.

Jalapeño Jelly

Yield: 16 cups

15 jalapeño peppers, red if
   possible, not seeded
5 red bell peppers, seeded
13 cups sugar

3 cups distilled vinegar
3 boxes (6 oz. each) Certo
   liquid pectin

Finely chop the jalapeño and red bell peppers in a food processor. In a heavy saucepan, combine peppers, sugar and vinegar. Bring to a boil for 3 minutes, then cool for 8 minutes. Skim and discard the foam on top of the jelly. Add pectin and bring back to a boil for 1 minute. Place in sterilized glass jars to cool. Refrigerate once jelly has cooled.

Chocolate Black Walnut Pie

Preparation Time: 1 Hour
Pre-heat oven to 375°

   3 large eggs
1½ cups sugar
   6 Tbsps. butter, melted
   2 Tbsps. vanilla extract
  ¾ cup flour
1½ cups semi-sweet chocolate chips
1½ cups black walnuts, chopped
   1 unbaked pie shell, chilled

Break eggs into a bowl and whip lightly. Continue to whip while adding sugar, butter and vanilla. Stir in flour, chocolate chips and walnuts.

Fill pie shell and bake 40 to 45 minutes at 375° until filling is fairly firm and crust is lightly browned. Chill.

Serve with vanilla ice cream or whipped cream.

STARS

AMERICAN
150 Redwood Alley
861-7827
Lunch 11:30AM–2:30pm Monday–Friday
Brunch 11AM Sunday
Dinner 5:30PM Wednesday–Sunday, 6:00PM Monday & Tuesday
AVERAGE DINNER FOR TWO: $80

Since its opening in 1984, Stars has been the stomping ground for the crème de la crème in film, comedy, politics, music and theater. Celebrities gather at San Francisco's longest bar to enjoy a cocktail or enjoy a meal in one of the two elevated dining rooms, decorated with brass railings and an appropriate star-patterned carpet. Chef/owner, Jeremiah Tower has synthesized food, wine and socializing to create the energetic ambiance of the restaurant.

Creative but traditional American cuisine celebrates the richer side of eating, using only the freshest ingredients. The menu changes nightly and a bar menu offers lighter fare, with most dishes cooked in a wood burning-oven.

Some notable appetizers include the Hawaiian Tuna Tartare. This mound of ahi tuna is roughly chopped and topped with green cilantro aioli and placed on rice noodles and chili-spiked red cabbage. The creamy Malpeque Oysters is always fresh and served with a mignonette.

Entrées include Roast Salmon with Risotto, Baby Turnips and Truffled Artichoke Sauce and Roasted Quail with Potato Risotto and served with sautéed spinach, shiitake, porcini and chanterelle mushrooms.

The desserts are artfully and deliciously prepared by pastry chef Emily Luchetti, so leave room for her Regina di Noci, an almond chocolate torte with espresso ice cream or a Grand Marnier soufflé with chocolate custard sauce.

Chef Jeremiah Tower's Menu for Four

Cream of Corn Soup with Crayfish Butter
Warm Cabbage Salad with Duck Fat
Braised Lamb Shanks
Grilled Squab Marinated in Berry Purée
Sponge Cake (recipe by Emily Luchetti)

Cream of Corn Soup with Crayfish Butter

Preparation Time: 25 Minutes

 8 **ears fresh corn**
 2 **Tbsps. butter**
½ **Tbsp. fresh marjoram leaves**
 2 **cups chicken stock**
¼ **cup crayfish or shellfish essence**
1½ **cups heavy cream**
   Salt & freshly ground pepper

Shuck the corn, remove all the silk from the ears, and slice downward on the ears between the cob and the kernels to remove the kernels without getting any of the cob.

Melt the butter in a saucepan and add the corn, marjoram and a few tablespoons of the stock. Cover and sweat over very low heat for 5 minutes. Boil the remaining stock and pour over the corn. Bring the corn back to a boil and remove from heat. As soon as it is cool enough to handle, purée it through the fine-mesh disk of a food mill or in a food processor, then press it through a sieve.

Whip the crayfish essence and ½ cup of cream to soft peaks.

When you are ready to serve, reheat the corn purée with the remaining cream. Check the seasoning and pour into soup plates. Spoon the shellfish cream onto the center of the soup.

Warm Cabbage Salad with Duck Fat

Serves 4
Preparation Time: 20 Minutes
Pre-heat oven to 350°

1 red cabbage
8 slices bacon or pancetta
8 slices white bread, preferably baguette or country bread
½ cup walnut halves
1 garlic clove, peeled, cut in half
2 Tbsps. red wine vinegar or fresh lemon juice
  Salt & freshly ground pepper
¼ cup rendered duck fat
4 one-ounce rounds of fresh white goat cheese
1 Tbsp. fresh parsley, chopped

Cut the cabbage in half through the root end. Cut out the core from each half. Turn the halves cut side down and slice crosswise into ⅛" pieces.

Lay the bacon out flat on a rack and bake or grill until crisp. When cool enough to handle, cut into 1" lengths. Keep warm.

Bake the bread crouton slices and walnuts on a sheet pan for 10 minutes. When the bread is cool enough to handle, rub with garlic. Keep the croutons warm and let the walnuts cool.

Put the cabbage in a bowl. Add the vinegar or lemon juice and the salt and pepper and toss the cabbage thoroughly.

Heat the duck fat in a pan and add the cabbage. Toss quickly but thoroughly for 30 seconds. Add the bacon and walnuts and toss again for 1 minute.

Serve immediately on warm plates. Place the cheese in the center of the cabbage, sprinkle with parsley and top with croutons.

Braised Lamb Shanks

Serves 4
Preparation Time: 2½ Hours
Pre-heat oven to 300°

4 lamb shanks
Salt and freshly ground
pepper
12 garlic cloves, unpeeled
6 bay leaves
6 sprigs fresh thyme
1 cup fresh mint leaves
½ Tbsp. fresh rosemary
leaves

1 qt. chicken, lamb, veal
or beef stock
1 cup aioli
24 cloves garlic, peeled
1 each large red pepper
and yellow bell pepper,
julienne
1 Tbsp. fresh thyme or
marjoram leaves
1 Tbsp. butter

Season the lamb shanks heavily with salt and pepper and put them in a casserole or heavy pot with the unpeeled garlic, bay leaves and thyme sprigs. Brown over medium heat for 15 minutes, turning shanks every 3 minutes. Cover pot and cook at 300° until shanks are very tender, about 2 hours.

While the lamb is cooking, blanch the mint leaves in boiling water for 1 minute. Drain, squeeze dry and purée with the rosemary and 2 Tbsps. stock in a blender. There should be a slight texture of the leaves in the purée. Mix into the aioli and let sit to develop the flavors.

Remove the shanks when they are done and keep warm and covered. Pour the remaining stock into the cooking pot and bring to a boil, scraping loose any meat juices. The moment the stock boils, turn off the heat and skim off all the fat. Bring the stock back to a boil and reduce the liquid to 2 cups. Skim off any fat and strain. Put the garlic cloves in the stock and simmer until tender, about 15 minutes. Strain and reserve the garlic and stock separately.

Put the shanks, peeled garlic, peppers, stock, marjoram and a pinch of salt in a sauté pan. Cook over medium heat, turning the shanks a couple of times, until the peppers are tender, about 10 minutes.

Place the shanks on warm plates. Stir the butter into the peppers and season. Spoon the peppers and garlic cloves around the shanks. Spoon some aioli over the shanks and serve the rest separately.

Grilled Squab Marinated in Berry Purée

Serves 4
Preparation Time: 30 Minutes (note marinating time)

  4 **squabs, with livers and hearts**
2 ½ **cups fresh raspberries**
  ½ **lb. butter**
     Salt & freshly ground pepper
  4 **Tbsps. olive oil**
  ½ **lb. salt pork, cut into 1" pieces**
  1 **Tbsp. fresh thyme leaves, chopped**
 16 **mushrooms**
  2 **Tbsps. lemon juice**
  ½ **cup walnut oil**
  3 **bunches watercress**

Cut the backbones from the squabs. Flatten the birds and fold the wings under. Select 24 raspberries for garnish and purée the rest through a sieve. Divide the purée in half. Mix half with the butter, salt and pepper in a food processor and set aside. Stir 2 Tbsps. of the olive oil into the other half of the raspberry purée. Season the birds and cover with the raspberry-oil marinade. Marinate for 1 hour.

Meanwhile, blanch the salt pork, rinse, and drain. Trim the squab liver. Mix the remaining olive oil and the thyme and marinate the salt pork, livers, hearts and mushrooms for 45 minutes; then put them on skewers.

Start a charcoal fire or heat the broiler. Grill the squabs, breast side down, for 5 minutes, moving them to a cooler part of the grill if they begin to brown too fast. Turn the squabs and grill, cavity side down, until the breast meat feels firm to the touch, about 8 minutes. Don't overcook them; they are best still a little pink. Put them aside to rest for 5 minutes while you grill the skewers for 5 minutes, turning them often.

Mix salt and pepper with the lemon juice and whisk in the walnut oil. Dress the watercress and put it on warm plates. Put the squabs in the center of each plate and the skewers around. Dress the whole raspberries in the vinaigrette remaining in the bowl and scatter them around the plate. Put some of the raspberry butter on top of each bird and serve.

Sponge Cake

Preparation Time: 30 Minutes
Pre-heat oven to 350°

1¼ **cups flour**
2½ **tsps. baking powder**
   Pinch salt
 5 **large eggs, separated**
1¼ **cups sugar**
 5 **Tbsps. boiling water**
 1 **tsp. vanilla extract**
   An 11½" × 17½" jelly roll pan or sheet pan with 1" sides

Line the bottom of jelly roll pan with parchment paper.

Sift together the flour, baking powder and salt. Set aside.

Put the egg yolks and sugar in the bowl of an electric mixer. Using the whisk attachment, whip on high speed until thick and pale yellow. Reduce to medium speed and slowly add the water and the vanilla. Scrape the sides and bottom of the bowl. Return to high speed and continue whipping for about 5 minutes, until mixture is again thick and forms ribbons.

Fold the dry ingredients into the egg-sugar mixture.

Put the egg whites in a separate bowl of an electric mixer. With the clean whisk attachment, whip on high speed until soft peaks form. Fold half of the whipped whites into the batter and then fold in the remaining whites. Spread the batter evenly into the pan.

Bake the cake for about 15 minutes, until it is golden brown and springs back when lightly touched.

VICTOR'S

AMERICAN
WESTIN ST. FRANCIS
335 Powell Street
Union Square
956-7777
Dinner served daily 6PM–10:30PM
Sunday champagne buffet brunch 10AM–2:30PM
AVERAGE DINNER FOR TWO: $80

TOPPING THE TOWER on the 32nd floor of the prestigious St. Francis Hotel is Victor's, the award-winning dining room offering spectacular vistas of the city and bay.

Victor's has once again received the highly coveted Travel-Holiday Award of Excellence for Fine Dining, Wine Spectator's Grand Award honoring its wine list and the Epicurean Rendezvous Dining Award.

Chef Joel Rambaud's extensive background includes classic French, Italian and nouvelle cuisines. He has received acclaim at such noted restaurants as L'Orangerie in Los Angeles, La Caravelle in New York and The Savoy Hotel in London.

Chef Joel Rambaud's Menu for Four

Hot Avocado Soup
Dungeness Crab Salad
Loin of Lamb En Croute
Pannequet of Berries

Avocado Soup

Preparation Time: 25 Minutes

5 avocados
2 pts. heavy cream
2 oz. sherry
4 oz. crab meat, chopped
4 drops Tabasco sauce
Lea & Perrins Sauce to taste
Salt and pepper
2 egg yolks

Peel and mash avocados. Add cream, (reserving 4 oz. for glaze topping) chopped crab meat and sherry. Bring to a boil. Add Tabasco sauce, Lea & Perrins Sauce, salt and pepper to taste.

For the glaze, in a separate dish, whip 4 oz. reserved cream and egg yolks.

To serve, pour 1 tsp. glaze over each serving of soup and place under broiler until brown.

Dungeness Crab Salad

Preparation Time: 30 Minutes

   2 large leeks
   6 oz. Dungeness crab meat
1½ oz. fresh mayonnaise
   8 quail eggs, hard boiled
   1 oz. golden caviar
   1 oz. American caviar
   Sweet pimentos or tomatoes, cut in ¼" wide sticks
 32 pieces of chive, cut 2" long

Cook the leeks in salted water, cut in half lengthwise and drain very well.

Mix crab with mayonnaise. Stuff half leek with crab and fold to make a roll.

Cut quail egg in half, remove and discard egg yolk. Fill half with golden caviar and half with American caviar.

Place the leeks in the middle of the plate with a cross of tomatoes and chives on the center. Serve cold.

Loin of Lamb en Croute

Preparation Time: 45 Minutes
Pre-heat oven to 375°

   1 rack of lamb
   ½ lb. spinach, cooked
   ½ lb. mushrooms, chopped
   1 shallot, chopped
   1 lb. puff pastry
   Egg wash (1 egg white or yolk, beaten with 1 Tbsp. water)

   Remove the lamb loin from the lamb rack. Set the rack aside for the garlic sauce.

   In a hot frying pan, brown the lamb loin on all sides, turning so it is well-colored. Refrigerate the loin while preparing the pastry.

   Combine the spinach, mushrooms and shallot in a pan over low heat. Cook until the shallot and mushroom are limp and translucent.

   Roll the puff pastry about ⅓″ thick. Spread with spinach-mushroom mixture. Place the cold lamb loin on the bed of spinach. Fold the pastry around the meat and seal with a light touch of water. Turn folds to bottom and brush top with egg wash.

   Place in a 375° oven and bake for 20 minutes or until golden and evenly browned.

   Serve with the garlic sauce.

Garlic Sauce

Preparation Time: 25 Minutes

Bones from rack of lamb
1 head garlic, peeled, crushed
1 medium carrot, chopped
1 large stalk celery, chopped
1 medium onion, cut in chunks
3 oz. mushrooms
One bunch parsley
2 bay leaves
8 cups water
3 cups white wine
6 oz. garlic puree
2 Tbsps. butter

Chop the rack bones into short lengths.

In a large stew pot, brown the lamb bones with garlic, carrot, celery, onion, mushrooms, parsley and bay leaves. Stir to prevent burning. When well browned, drain off fat. Add water and boil until reduced by half. Add wine and reduce again by half. Add garlic pureé and set on low burner to simmer.

Serve with the Loin of Lamb En Croute.

Pannequet of Berries

Preparation Time: 45 Minutes (note refrigeration time)
Pre-heat oven to 400°

1¼ **cups whipping cream**
1¼ **cups lemon juice**
 ¼ **cup flour**
 1 **cup sugar**
 1 **egg yolk**
 1 **Tbsp. gelatin**
 5 **egg whites**
 ½ **cup berries**
   Parchment paper to line the mold

Make a pastry cream by bringing the cream and lemon juice to a boil over high heat. Add the flour, ¼ cup sugar and egg yolk. Bring back to a boil for a few minutes while stirring with a wire whip. Remove from heat and mix in gelatin. Set aside.

In a medium bowl beat egg whites and remaining ¾ cup sugar together, to make the meringue. Slowly fold the meringue into the cream mixture while still hot.

In a 1-inch mold, layer the berries and cream meringue mixture. Freeze until hard. Unmold, bake at 400° until golden brown.

Cooking tip: May be served with a fruit syrup of your choice.

Cafe Majestic

CALIFORNIAN
1500 Sutter Street at Gough
776-6400
Tuesday—Sunday 7AM—10PM
Brunch Saturday—Sunday 8AM—3PM
Monday breakfast 7AM—10:30AM
Piano entertainment nightly
AVERAGE DINNER FOR TWO: $45

A RESTAURANT THAT embodies the best of San Francisco, Cafe Majestic balances Victorian grandeur with contemporary vitality. Just off the lobby of the authentically restored Majestic Hotel, the dining room is elegantly romantic. Foam green wainscot and apricot walls are accented by graceful columns and large potted palms. Unusual cast-iron and oak chairs surround tables set with white linen, candles and flowers. Adjoining the restaurant is a 125-year-old bar, taken from a cafe in Paris, backed by mirrors and flanked by an arresting collection of butterflies. The creators of Cafe Majestic are Stanley Eichelbaum and Tom Marshall.

To complement the turn-of-the-century decor, the Majestic has taken recipes from early San Francisco restaurants and given them a modern interpretation. A perfect example of one of these classics is Chicken Nellie Melba, a grilled chicken topped with lychee nuts in a wild mushroom sauce. Or try a juicy veal chop crowned with fresh sage and melted fontina, surrounded by a garden assortment of vegetables and the crispiest shoestring potatoes in town.

Cafe Majestic is relaxed and lively enough to be the perfect spot for breakfast, lunch or weekend brunch, yet special enough for the most important dinner occasion.

Chef Ron Miller's Menu for Six

Pumpkin & Red Pepper Slippers
Warm Scallop & Prawn Salad with
Cranberry Dressing
Roast Turkey Breast with Corn, Sundried Cherries and
Wild Rice Stuffing
Majestic Tiramisú

Pumpkin and Red Pepper Slippers

Preparation Time: 45 Minutes
Pre-heat oven to 350°

6 small red bell peppers (Anaheim red or Pasilla)
3 cups cooked pumpkin squash
1 Tbsp. nutmeg
¼ cup hazelnuts, chopped
5 Tbsps. shallots, chopped
5 Tbsps. fresh ginger, chopped
2 Tbsps. honey
1 Tbsp. cinnamon
½ tsp. salt
½ tsp. white pepper
¼ cup sherry
6 sprigs watercress

Place bell peppers on sheetpan, hollowed out, and with tops that still have the stem sliced off at an angle, like the top of a shoe.

In a large bowl combine the squash, nutmeg, hazelnuts, 3 Tbsps. shallots, 2 Tbsps. ginger, honey, cinnamon, salt and pepper. Stuff each pepper with the squash mixture and brush with salad oil for a fine glossy finish. Bake at 350° for 20 minutes.

Sprinkle 3 Tbsps. ginger and 2 Tbsps. shallots onto pan after roasting peppers. Deglaze with sherry. Pour over each slipper and garnish with watercress.

Warm Scallop and Prawn Salad with Radicchio & Tangerines

Preparation Time: 25 Minutes

12 scallops
12 prawns
 2 cups white wine
    Bay leaf
 ½ medium onion
 1 lemon
 4 tangerines
 3 heads radicchio, chopped
 1 bunch chives, chopped

Poach scallops and prawns in white wine with bay leaf, onion, zest of lemon and zest of tangerine for 5 minutes or until done.

Place shellfish on a bed of radicchio. Ladle dressing to one side and garnish with tangerine slices and tangerine sections. Sprinkle chives on top.

Cranberry Dressing

Preparation Time: 5 Minutes

 2 Tbsps. shallots
 ½ cup cranberries
    Tangerine zest
 ¾ cup cranberry juice
 2 Tbsps. sherry vinegar
    Salt and pepper to taste
 1 cup lowfat yogurt

In a saucepan combine shallots, cranberries, tangerine zest, cranberry juice, vinegar, salt and pepper. Bring to a boil and reduce by half. Remove from heat and whisk in yogurt.

Roast Turkey Breast with Corn, Sundried Cherries and Wild Rice Stuffing

Preparation Time: 1½ hours
Pre-heat oven to 375°

One 3 lb. turkey breast
2 cups chicken or turkey
  broth
¼ cup celery, chopped
¼ cup onion, chopped
¼ cup leeks, chopped
½ cup fresh corn
½ cup brown rice, cooked

½ cup wild rice, cooked
½ cup bread crumbs
1 egg white
1 sprig thyme, chopped
  Salt and pepper to taste
¼ cup sundried cherries
½ cup pecans, chopped
¼ cup mustard

Blanch celery, onion and leek in 1 cup turkey or chicken broth. Cook corn in broth until done. Add brown and wild rice, bread crumbs, egg white, seasonings, cherries and ¼ cup pecans.

Butterfly the turkey breast and remove the skin. Stuff with mixture and tie together with a string. Brush turkey with mustard and coat with ¼ cup crushed pecans.

Roast at 375° for 1 hour or until done. Baste with turkey broth instead of butter.

Sauce

3 cups chicken or turkey stock
¼ cup port wine
¼ cup sundried cherries (raisins may be substituted)
2 Tbsps. jalapeños

Deglaze roasting pan with turkey stock, port wine, sundried cherries and jalapeños. Reduce to sauce-like consistency.

Majestic Tiramisú

Preparation Time: 30 Minutes

½ **cup semi-sweet chocolate**
¾ **cup heavy cream**
26 **ladyfingers**
2 **cups mascarpone cheese**
½ **cup sugar**
¼ **cup dark rum**
1 **cup espresso**
Garnish of chocolate shavings

Make the ganache by melting chocolate with ½ cup cream. Do not bring to a boil

Spread ganache on 15 ladyfingers to form sandwiches

Whip cheese, sugar, rum and remaining cream until spreadable. Do not overwhip. Set aside.

Dip ladyfinger sandwiches in espresso to soak. Squeeze out excess liquid.

Working quickly, lay end to end 4 sandwiches on serving plate, frost with a layer of cheese and repeat. Completely frost cake. Adhere remaining ladyfingers, which have been cut in half, around cake.

Garnish with chocolate shavings.

San Francisco City Hall in 1906; it took the earthquake only 20 seconds to make a total wreck of it.

GREENS

CALIFORNIAN
Fort Mason
Building A
771-7955
Lunch Tuesday–Saturday 11:30AM–2:15PM
Dinner Tuesday–Saturday 6PM–9:30PM
Brunch Sunday 10AM–2PM
AVERAGE DINNER FOR TWO: $40

GREENS AT FORT MASON was opened in 1979 to offer lively and enjoyable vegetarian food to a public accustomed to eating meat. The menu offers a wide variety of cooking styles from southern France and Italy, dishes from Mexico and the American Southwest and a few adaptations from the cuisines of Asia.

The setting is ideal. The large dining room sits on a dock that juts into San Francisco Bay. A wall of glass faces the Golden Gate Bridge and the hills of the Marin headlands.

Foghorns, ships' bells, and seagulls fill the air with sound, and often, as dinner begins, the setting sun floods the dining room with light.

greens
AT FORT MASON

Butternut Squash & Leek Soup with Gruyere Cheese
Pear & Walnut Salad
Grilled Vegetables with Port Beurre Rouge
Winter Vegetable Ragout with Soft Polenta
Italian Plum Almond Tart

Pear & Walnuts with Romaine Hearts, Watercress & Radicchio

Preparation Time: 15 Minutes
Pre-heat oven to 375°

½ cup walnuts, chopped
2 heads romaine lettuce
1 small head radicchio
2 bunches watercress
2 ripe Comice pears, cored
and sliced

Walnut-sherry vinaigrette
(see below)
Freshly-ground black
pepper

Toast walnuts for 10 minutes, until they begin to brown. Set aside to cool. Prepare salad greens. Rinse the greens and spin dry. Toss the salad greens, pears and walnuts with walnut-sherry vinaigrette. Sprinkle with black pepper and serve.

Walnut Sherry Vinaigrette

3 Tbsps. sherry vinegar
1 small shallot, minced
Salt to taste

4 Tbsps. light olive oil
4 Tbsps. walnut oil

Combine the vinegar, salt and shallot. Whisk in the oils to emulsify. Pour over greens and toss.

Cooking tip: This salad is a fall and winter favorite. If watercress or radicchio are not available, substitute chicory, escarole or other bitter greens.

Butternut Squash & Leek Soup with Gruyere Cheese & Thyme

2 Tbsps. butter
  Whites of 2 medium leeks,
    sliced
4 cloves garlic, minced
  Salt to taste
½ tsp. dried thyme

½ cup white wine
2 medium butternut squash
  Black or white pepper
¼ lb. Gruyere cheese, grated
1 small bunch fresh thyme,
  chopped

Melt the butter in a thick-bottomed soup pot. Add the leeks, garlic, salt and thyme. Cook the leeks until tender. Add the wine and cook until the wine has reduced.

Peel, seed and cut the squash into small cubes, approximately 4 cups. Add the cubed squash to the soup and cover with stock. Cook over medium heat until the squash takes on a rather smooth consistency. Thin the soup with more stock if necessary, to desired consistency. Season to taste with salt and pepper. Sprinkle with grated Gruyere cheese and chopped fresh thyme.

Soup Stock

Tops of 2 medium leeks,
  chopped
1 carrot, peeled and
  chopped
1 medium potato, chopped
2 celery stalks, chopped
2 bay leaves
1 Tbsp. fresh marjoram

1 Tbsp. fresh oregano
1 Tbsp. fresh thyme
1 Tbsp. fresh parsley
4 cloves garlic
  Two black peppercorns
  Pinch of salt
5 cups cold water

Combine all ingredients in a large pot. Cover with cold water and cook over moderate heat until the stock begins to boil. Turn down the heat and simmer for 30 minutes. Strain stock and discard cooked vegetables.

Cooking note: Any flavorful winter squash can be substituted for butternut.

Grilled Vegetables with Port Beurre Rouge

Preparation Time: 25 Minutes
Pre-heat oven to 375°

2 lbs. Delicata squash or any edible-skin squash
1 lb. shiitake mushrooms
1 bunch scallions
¼ cup olive oil
1 clove garlic, finely diced
  Salt and freshly-ground black pepper
  Bamboo skewers for mushrooms

Be sure to select a thin-skinned winter squash for this dish. Wash squash, trim off ends and cut into ¾" thick rounds. Scoop seeds out of each round. Place squash rounds on a lightly oiled baking sheet.

Combine oil and garlic and brush over squash. Sprinkle with salt and pepper.

Bake until just tender, about 15 minutes. Do not overbake, as it needs to be firm enough to hold its shape on the grill.

Stem shiitake mushrooms. Discard stems. Do not wash shiitakes. If dirty, brush with a damp cloth.

Skewer shiitakes and brush with garlic oil, salt and pepper.

Trim root hairs off scallions. Pull away outer membrane on white end of scallions. Trim away most of the scallion green, so it is about 6" in length. Brush with garlic oil, salt and pepper.

Grill or broil the squash rounds, shiitake and scallions. Allow 6 minutes to cook vegetables, turning them after 3 minutes.

Serve with port beurre rouge.

Port Beurre Rouge

Preparation Time: 15 Minutes
Yield: 1 Cup

¼ cup balsamic vinegar
¼ cup port
2 shallots, diced
½ lb. cold butter, cut into ½" cubes
Salt and freshly-ground black pepper

Combine vinegar, port and shallots in a saucepan. Cook over high heat until most of the liquid has reduced. Watch the pan closely, as it is easy to burn the reduction in the last minutes of cooking. Turn heat down to moderate and slowly whisk in the butter cubes. Add a few pieces at a time, whisking until all the butter is incorporated.

Remove pan from heat and season with salt and pepper. Add a few splashes of balsamic vinegar if sauce needs more sharpness.

Ladle sauce onto a serving platter and arrange grilled vegetables on it.

Cooking tip: Port beurre rouge is a favorite fall and winter sauce for grilled vegetables. The sweetness of the port and balsamic vinegar are very pleasing and the color of the sauce is dramatic. People tend to shy away from butter sauces, but we have found them to be quite easy. This sauce is definitely worth the effort. It can be made ahead of time, as long as it is kept in a warm, but not hot place.

Mushroom & Winter Vegetable Ragout with Soft Polenta

Preparation Time: One Hour

Quick Mushroom Stock

3 oz. dried shiitake
    mushrooms
A few sprigs of fresh herbs
½ medium yellow onion,
    sliced

4 cloves garlic
2 cups cold water
¼ cup soy sauce
Pinch of salt

Combine all ingredients and bring to a boil. Simmer over low heat while cooking the polenta. Cook for 30 minutes, strain stock and discard vegetables.

Soft Polenta

1 cup polenta
4 cups boiling salted
    water
¼ cup butter

Salt and black pepper to
    taste
½ lb. Parmesan cheese,
    grated

Allow 20 minutes to cook the polenta. It can be easily done while cooking the stock.

Whisk polenta into boiling water and continue to whisk vigorously until polenta dissolves. Turn down the heat and continue to stir so polenta does not stick to the bottom of the pan. Cook over medium heat until the grains dissolve completely and the polenta is smooth, approximately 20 minutes. Add butter, salt and pepper.

When the polenta is done, leave over low flame and stir occasionally until ready to serve. Thin with hot water if it begins to thicken.

Add half of the cheese just before serving and sprinkle the rest of the cheese over the polenta when it is served.

Ragout

1 medium yellow onion, diced large
2 Tbsps. butter
2 Tbsps. olive oil
4 cloves garlic, minced
   Salt and freshly-ground black pepper
1 cup red wine
1 lb. mushrooms, sliced thick
1 large turnip, cut into ½" cubes
2 fennel bulbs, sliced thick
1 medium red pepper, sliced thick
1 medium yellow pepper, sliced thick
   Soy sauce to taste
1½ cup fresh herbs (parsley, marjoram, oregano, chives)
¼ cup sour cream or creme fraiche

Sauté onion in butter and olive oil with garlic and salt and pepper until soft. Add half of the wine and reduce. Add the mushrooms, followed by the turnips, fennel and peppers. Season with a few splashes of soy sauce. Add more butter and olive oil as necessary, the remaining wine, and just enough mushroom stock to make a sauce. Cook the vegetables until tender and flavorful. Be careful not to overcook the ragout, as the vegetables should be tender, yet firm. Finish seasoning with fresh herbs, salt and pepper. Add creme fraiche or sour cream to lightly bind the sauce. Serve with soft polenta.

Cooking tip: Mushrooms that work well in this dish are fresh shiitake, chanterelle or porcini mushrooms. If using fresh shiitake mushrooms, use only the caps for the ragout.

Italian Plum Almond Tart

Preparation Time: One Hour
Pre-heat oven to 375°

Almond Pastry Shell

1 cup all-purpose flour
2 Tbsps. sugar
  Pinch of salt

¼ cup almond paste
6 Tbsps. cold butter
1 egg yolk

Put flour, sugar, salt, and almond paste in food processor bowl and pulse until blended.

Cut butter into small pieces and add to mixture. Pulse again until mixture is blended. Add egg yolk and pulse briefly until dough holds together when pinched.

Press dough into 9″ tart pan and bake until lightly brown. Set aside and cool.

Almond Filling

1 cup sliced almonds
1 egg
1 yolk
⅓ cup sugar
½ tsp. orange zest,
  grated

3 Tbsps. unsalted butter,
  melted
Plum liqueur or kirsch to
  taste
2 lbs. Italian prune plums,
  thinly sliced

Grind almonds finely in food processor. Beat egg yolk, sugar and zest. Mix in melted butter and ground almonds. Add liqueur to taste.

Arrange plums on bottom of tart shell. Cover with almond filling, spreading with a spatula.

Bake at 350° for 40 to 45 minutes, or until filling is set.

SILKS

CALIFORNIAN
MANDARIN ORIENTAL HOTEL
222 Sansome Street
986-2020
Breakfast Monday–Saturday 7AM–10:30
Lunch Monday–Friday 11:30AM–2:00PM
Dinner daily 6PM–10PM
Sunday Brunch 8AM–2PM
AVERAGE DINNER FOR TWO: $60–$70

SILKS IS LOCATED in the Mandarin Oriental, one of San Francisco's finest internationally renowned hotels. Situated in a grand Oriental setting, Silks is an elegant restaurant offering a contemporary blend of California cooking with Asian accents.

The atmosphere is romantic with soft pastel coloring, watercolors painted on silk and framed in 18 karat gold leaf frames, upholstered arm chairs and lush floral arrangements.

San Francisco Focus Magazine recently awarded Silks a gold for "Best Service," a silver for "Best Hotel Restaurant," and a bronze for "Best Restaurant in the Bay Area."

Chef Richard Hauff's Menu for Six

Butternut Squash & Pear Soup
Mixed Greens with Lemon-Miso Dressing
Coriander Cured Salmon with Spicy Cucumbers
Grilled Chicken, Japanese Style
Flourless Chocolate Cake

Butternut Squash & Pear Soup

Preparation Time: 1 Hour 10 Minutes

1 medium onion, peeled, sliced thinly
2 ribs celery, sliced thinly
2 cloves garlic, peeled, crushed
2 oz. whole butter, unsalted
1 medium butternut squash, peeled, seeded, diced
2 French butter pears, peeled, halved, seeded
4 cups chicken stock or vegetable broth
1 cup heavy cream
   Salt and pepper to taste

Sauté onions, celery and garlic in butter until soft. Add squash and pears and cover with the stock. Simmer, stirring occasionally until squash is soft.

Puree soup in a food processor or blender until smooth. Return to pot. Add cream and adjust seasonings with salt and pepper.

Cooking tip: This makes an excellent sauce for grilled shrimp or lobster.

Mixed Seasonal Greens with Lemon-Miso Dressing

Preparation Time: 15 Minutes

    1 Tbsp. white miso
    3 Tbsps. lemon juice
1½ Tbsps. rice vinegar
    2 shallots, finely diced
 ½ cup peanut oil
 ¼ cup extra virgin olive oil
    2 Tbsps. water
      Salt and fresh pepper

In a stainless steel bowl, whisk thoroughly together the miso, lemon juice, rice vinegar and shallots.

Slowly incorporate both oils, whisking briskly so the sauce is emulsified.

Thin down with small amounts of tepid water.

Season with salt and pepper.

Gently toss mixed seasonal greens with the lemon-miso dressing and serve.

Cooking tip: Be careful of salt, because the saltiness of miso varies.

Coriander Cured Salmon with Spicy Cucumbers

Preparation Time: 2 Hours (note refrigeration time)

14 oz. filet of salmon,
   boneless
Pepper
2 cups kosher salt

6 Tbsps. sugar
5 Tbsps. coriander seed,
   crushed

Pepper the salmon liberally on all sides. Mix salt, sugar and coriander seeds and coat salmon in this dry mix. Cover with plastic wrap, refrigerate and weigh down lightly with a plate. After 12 hours, the texture will be the same as smoked salmon. Wash lightly and pat dry. Wrap tightly in plastic wrap and refrigerate.

Cucumber Salad

1 English cucumber
1 Tbsp. kosher salt
1 cup rice vinegar
2 Tbsps. Mirin (Japanese
   cooking wine)
2 Tbsps. lime juice

¼ cup sesame oil
2 tsps. jalepeño peppers,
   seeded, diced
Pepper
1 Tbsp. black sesame seeds,
   toasted

Quarter cucumbers lengthwise and slice out small wedge of seeds. Cut into small pieces ¼" thick. Place cucumbers in a colander and mix thoroughly with the salt. Season the cucumbers with vinegar, Mirin, lime juice, sesame oil and peppers. Adjust seasonings with fresh ground pepper and salt if necessary.

To assemble, place a mound of cucumber salad in center of plate. Slice the fish very thinly and place around cucumbers. Sprinkle with sesame seeds.

Grilled Chicken, Japanese Style with Fennel, Leek and Radish

Preparation Time: 1 ½ Hours

2 chickens
1¼ cups sake
 ½ cup Mirin (Japanese
      cooking wine)
 2 cups sugar
 1 cup brown sugar
 ½ cup honey
 3 Tbsps. tamari
 2 medium sized leeks
 2 fennel bulbs
 1 bunch radishes
 4 oz. butter, unsalted

Cut the chicken into breasts, thighs and legs. Grill in a medium to hot charcoal fire, making sure that the skin is very crisp. Do not baste the chicken with the sauce until 3 minutes before the chicken is done.

In a stainless steel pot, combine the sake, Mirin, sugars, honey and tamari. Simmer the sauce, skim and reduce by 20%. Strain.

Cut the greens off the leeks and quarter to the root. Cut into ½" squares.

Cut the fennel bulbs in half lengthwise and julienne.

Slice the radishes into thin rounds.

Blanch the leeks and fennel for 10 seconds in boiling salted water. Refresh in ice water. Combine the leeks and fennel with the radish. Heat the vegetables in ¼ cup water and butter. Season with salt and pepper.

Place vegetables on a serving plate with grilled chicken pieces on top.

Flourless Chocolate Cake

Preparation Time: 45 Minutes
Pre-heat oven to 375°

- 7 oz. sugar
- 3 egg whites, room temperature
- 3 yolks and 1 egg
- 7 oz. bittersweet chocolate
- 7 oz. butter, unsalted
-   Pinch of salt
-   Garnish of powdered sugar and/or cocoa

Combine ⅓ of sugar with the egg whites and whip to a soft peak. Set aside.

Combine remaining sugar with the yolks and 1 egg. Beat until color lightens and forms a ribbon.

Melt chocolate, butter and salt over a double boiler.

In a large bowl, combine the chocolate with the yolk mixture until blended. Fold in the egg white mixture and pour into a 9″ cake round.

Bake at 375° for 25 minutes or until a toothpick comes out clean. Unmold after cake is cool.

Garnish with powdered sugar and/or cocoa.

SQUARE ONE RESTAURANT

CALIFORNIA CUISINE
190 Pacific Avenue at Front
788-1110
Lunch Monday—Friday 11:30AM—2:30PM
Dinner Monday—Thursday 5:30—10PM
Friday—Saturday 5:30—10:30PM
Sunday 5—9:30PM
AVERAGE DINNER FOR TWO: $70

THE NAME, SQUARE ONE, implies fresh beginnings. Here, everything served is prepared daily, including two breads, pasta, pastries, ice creams and sorbets, chutney and preserves.

Under the direction of Chef Joyce Goldstein, the menu changes every day, offering an international repertoire of recipes, with an emphasis on dishes of Mediterranean origin. Homemade soups, pastas, assorted salads, meats, fish and poultry, not to mention wonderful desserts are featured.

Square One Restaurant has a complete bar with award-winning wine list of both domestic and imported vintages.

This is a restaurant that is informal in spirit but elegant in food preparation and visual design. As Gourmet Magazine said in its review, "Square One is a restaurant run by people who really love to cook for people who love to eat."

SQUARE ONE

Chef Joyce Goldstein's Menu for Four

Smoked Trout Paté
Pea and Lettuce Soup
Fattoush
Grilled Chicken in Five Spice Marinade
Caramel Pot de Creme

Smoked Trout Paté

Preparation Time: 15 Minutes

1½ lbs. smoked trout
  ½ cup white or yellow onion,
    finely diced
  ½ cup chives, chopped

1 cup mayonnaise
  Salt and pepper to taste
  Lemon juice to taste

Remove the heads and skin from the trout and bone carefully, to yield ½ pound of smoked filets after cleaning. Put the trout in a food processor and pulse until chopped. Transfer to a bowl and fold in the rest of the ingredients.

Mayonnaise

3 egg yolks
¼ cup lemon juice
2 cups mild olive oil, not virgin

Blend yolks and lemon juice until creamy. Slowly add the oil until desired consistency.

Cooking tip: This is a wonderful spread for croutons, tastes good on avocados and makes a rich sandwich spread when paired with sliced cucumbers and watercress on dark rye or pumpernickel bread.

Pea and Lettuce Soup

Preparation Time: 25 Minutes

   2 Tbsps. unsalted butter
   1 cup yellow onion, diced
   4 cups shelled peas
2½ cups chicken stock
   3 tightly-packed cups lettuce, julienned
      Salt and pepper to taste
      Pinch of sugar, optional

   Melt the butter in a medium size saucepan over moderate heat. Add the onions and cook for about 8-10 minutes, until tender and translucent. Add the peas and 2 cups of the stock, bring to a full boil. Lower heat and simmer for 5 minutes, or until the peas are tender. Add the lettuce and cook for 2 minutes until the lettuce is wilted.

   Puree the soup in a blender or food processor. Thin with the remaining stock to the desired consistency.

   Season the soup to taste with salt and pepper. If the peas are a bit starchy, add a pinch of sugar for balance.

Cooking tip: For the lettuce you may use romaine, butter or an assortment of greens. You do not need much stock. As the lettuce cooks, it gives off quite a bit of liquid. For a garnish, you might try a mint cream or a lemon cream and diced prosciutto or fried bread croutons.

Fattoush
(Lebanese Toasted Pita Bread Salad)

Preparation Time: 15 Minutes

  4 whole round pieces of pita bread
  2 cups tomato, diced
  2 cups cucumber, diced
  8 Tbsps. red onion, chopped fine
  8 Tbsps. green onions, chopped fine
  8 tsps. mint, chopped
  8 tsps. parsley, chopped
  4 cups romaine lettuce, julienned, loosely packed
10 oz. vinaigrette (recipe follows)
   Salt and pepper to taste

Toast the pita bread until it is semi-crisp. Then break it up into 2″ pieces. Do not crumble.

The tomato or cucumbers do not need to be peeled. Remove the cucumber seeds if they are very seedy.

Toss the romaine with vinaigrette and place it on the salad plate. Toss the diced vegetables, mint, parsley and pita pieces with vinaigrette and mound this mixture on top of the romaine.

Citrus Vinaigrette

10 Tbsps. olive oil
 3 Tbsps. lemon juice
  Salt and pepper

Blend ingredients well. This may become your favorite summer salad!

Grilled Chicken in a Spicy Oriental Five Spice Marinade

Preparation Time: 30 Minutes (note refrigeration time)

6 lbs. chicken, butterflied or half broilers
2 cups olive oil
3 Tbsps. red pepper flakes
  Zest of 3 large oranges
6 cloves garlic, smashed
  Six 2" thick pieces peeled ginger root, mashed
2 Tbsps. five spice powder
⅛ cup sesame oil
¼ cup fresh lemon juice
  Salt

Heat the olive oil in a medium saucepan. Add the red pepper flakes, orange zest, garlic and ginger. After 10 minutes add the remaining ingredients. Cool completely.

Pour the marinade over the chicken. Cover and refrigerate overnight. Bring to room temperature before broiling or grilling. Broil 4 minutes on each side.

Five Spice Powder

Equal parts in weight of cinnamon sticks, star anise, cloves, fennel seed and black peppercorns. Grind in spice mill. Can be stored for a few months at room temperature, in a tightly sealed jar.

Caramel Pot de Creme

Preparation Time: One hour
Pre-heat oven to 300°

2 cups milk
2 cups heavy cream
1 vanilla bean, cut in half

1 cup sugar
12 egg yolks

Scald the milk and cream with the vanilla bean. Keep the mixture warm.

In a heavy-bottomed saucepan caramelize the sugar until it is a deep amber hue. Strain the warm cream and gradually and carefully add it into the caramel, whisking constantly. Be careful, as the caramel will foam up.

In a mixing bowl combine the sugar and yolks and gradually add the hot caramel cream. Strain again.

Ladle or gently pour the mixture into 8 ramekins. Skim the top surfaces to remove all bubbles.

Place the ramekins into a pan of hot water and cover the pan with foil. Bake for 40 minutes or until the custard is set. Remove from water and cool. Cover with plastic wrap and refrigerate. Bring to room temperature before serving. Top with the following caramel sauce.

Caramel Sauce

2 cups sugar
Juice of half lemon

1 cup heavy cream
8 Tbsps. unsalted butter

Combine sugar and lemon juice and cook the syrup over medium heat. Caramelize until golden brown.

In another pot, heat the cream. Gradually add the cream to the caramelized sugar while stirring. Bring to a boil and stir in butter.

Pour the mixture into a heat-proof container.

Refrigerate. Heat it over hot water before using.

GEVA'S

CARIBBEAN
482-A Hayes Street
863-1220
Lunch Tuesday–Friday 11:30AM–2:30PM
Dinner Tuesday–Sunday 5:30PM–10:30PM
Sunday brunch 11AM–3PM
AVERAGE DINNER FOR TWO: $30

CONTEMPORARY CARIBBEAN CUISINE inspired by West Indian culinary traditions best describes Geva's spicy Jamaican cooking. The food is fresh and well seasoned, offering tempting delicacies such as the jalapeño-hot pepperpot soup with chunks of crabmeat, and the stamp and go—codfish fritters with a hot salsa. Some of the house specialties include jerk chicken in a garlic ginger sauce, curried goat, Caribbean fish stew, calypso stir fry and scallop salad with pesto.

Reggae music sets the mood in this extremely popular cafe. Geva's coral-colored interior is tastefully decorated with fresh flowers, white tablecloths and island-family photographs on the wall. French doors open onto a patio.

This is island cooking at its best!

Chef Icilda Vincent's Menu for Eight

Jerk Chicken Drumettes
Shrimp Salad with Tomatoes
Lime Garlic Shrimp
Curried Goat
Sweet Potato Pone

Jerk Chicken

Preparation Time: 25 Minutes (note marinating time)

3 lbs. chicken drumettes
4 oz. oil
5 oz. Jerk seasoning*
1 scallion, cored

Coat chicken with oil. Add jerk seasoning and mix. Marinate 4 hours.

Grill on low flame. Garnish with the white part of the scallion.

*Jerk seasoning can be purchased in any specialty food store or Jamaican store.

Shrimp Salad with Tomatoes

Preparation Time: 25 Minutes

2½ lbs. medium shrimp (21–25)
  2 Tbsps. salt
  2 Tbsps. black pepper
  4 oz. soft cream cheese
½ cup mayonnaise
  1 Tbsp. Dijon mustard
½ tsp. hot sauce
  2 Tbsps. lemon juice
  2 cups celery, finely chopped
  1 cup onion, finely chopped
  2 lbs. tomatoes
  Green leaves for garnish
  2 lemons, sliced

Cover shrimp in water and bring to a low boil. When the shrimp are pink, remove from the heat. Rinse with cold water. Clean and devein the shrimp. Add salt and pepper. Refrigerate.

Blend the cream cheese and mayonnaise in a large bowl. Add mustard, hot sauce and lemon juice, mixing well. Add the celery, onions and shrimp.

Slice tomatoes in round ⅛" slices.

Place green leaves on plate's edge with tomato slices. Mound shrimp salad in middle and garnish with lemon slices.

Lime Garlic Shrimp

Preparation Time: 15 Minutes

3 lbs. medium shrimp
¼ cup butter + 2 Tbsps.
4 cloves garlic, minced
1 cup onions, minced
2 tsps. ginger, minced
   Coarsely ground black pepper
¼ cup white wine
¼ cup lime juice (2 limes)
1 strawberry, sliced
½ cup fresh parsley, chopped

Clean shrimp and set aside.

Melt butter and sauté the garlic, onions, ginger and pepper for 30 seconds on medium heat. Add shrimp and white wine. Add lime juice and 2 Tbsps. butter. Cook 1 minute.

Garnish with strawberry slices and parsley.

Cooking tip: Lime Garlic Shrimp can be served as an entree with rice and vegetables.

Curried Goat

Preparation Time: 35 Minutes (note marinating time)

6½ lb. goat meat, cubed
  2 Tbsps. salt
  2 Tbsps. black pepper
  ¼ tsp. allspice
  ¼ cup curry powder
  2 cloves garlic, chopped
  1 tsp. cayenne pepper
  1 onion, chopped
  ¼ cup oil
  2 cups beef stock
  2 white potatoes, cubed
  ½ cup coconut cream
    Garnish with shredded coconut flakes, optional

Bone and trim fat from meat. Season meat with salt, pepper, allspice, curry powder, garlic, cayenne pepper and onions. Marinate for 1 hour.

Heat oil in a large sauce pan and cook the meat for 5 minutes. Add stock, marinating seasonings and potatoes. Cook until the meat is tender. Add coconut cream and simmer 15 minutes.

Add more pepper seasoning if you want to make it spicier. Garnish with coconut flakes. Serve hot.

Cooking tip: Chutney is a good accompaniment to this dish.

Sweet Potato Pone

Preparation Time: 1 Hour, 15 Minutes
Pre-heat oven to 350°

2 lbs. raw sweet potatoes, peeled, grated
1 cup milk
1 cup cream of coconut
1¼ cups brown sugar
1 Tbsp. ground ginger
1 tsp. cinnamon
1 tsp. vanilla extract
½ tsp. nutmeg or mace
½ cup raisins
One 7oz. package dried coconut flakes
2 cups hot water
2 Tbsps. butter, melted
1 cup flour
1 pt. whipping cream
1 cup rum
Garnish with whipping cream

Mix all ingredients, except the garnish, in a large bowl. Transfer to a baking dish and bake for 1 hour.

Serve warm with whipped cream.

CHINA MOON CAFE

CHINESE
639 Post Street
775-4789
Dim-sum lunch served daily 11:30AM–2:15PM
Dinner daily 5:30–10PM
AVERAGE DINNER FOR TWO: $45–$50

AN ARRAY OF California-Chinese delicacies in a comfortable Art Deco setting best describes China Moon Cafe, one of San Francisco's most talked about dining establishments.

Famed for the uncompromising quality of its food and for the originality of chef/owner Barbara Tropp, China Moon Cafe is a cozy upscale haven where hearty conversation, great food and wine and expert service prevail.

House favorites include Peking antipasto platter with smoked or wok-seared meats, homemade pickled vegetables with bright salads of baby greens and pot-browned noodle pillows topped with tender poultry ribbons and fresh Chinese vegetables. Other goodies include crispy spring rolls stuffed with minced meats and fresh chiles, and a zesty fresh ginger ice cream drizzled with bittersweet chocolate sauce and served with a selection of seven miniature cookies.

Barbara is a Chinese scholar turned Chinese cook. She is the author of *The Modern Art of Chinese Cooking* and is currently working on *The China Moon Cookbook* (Workman Publishing) to be released in 1991. Barbara has shared some of the recipes from her forthcoming cookbook.

Chef Barbara Tropp's Menu for Six

Sweet Mama Squash Soup
Five-Spice Duck Breasts
Crunchy Red Cabbage Slaw
China Moon Pickled Ginger
Spicy Ginger Moons

Crunchy Red Cabbage Slaw

Copyright The China Moon Cookbook

Preparation Time: 15 Minutes (note refrigeration time)

1 lb. red cabbage
¾ cup pickled ginger juice
2 Tbsps. pickled ginger, minced
  Sugar and kosher salt to taste
  Garnish of toasted black sesame seeds
1 green scallion, sliced

At least 12 hours and ideally 2–3 days in advance, make the slaw. Taste the pickled ginger juice if you are using a commercial variety and adjust to your taste with sugar and salt. If you are using "China Moon Pickled Ginger," the flavors are already balanced.

Core the red cabbage and slice crosswise into fine shreds.

Combine the sliced cabbage, pickled ginger juice and pickled ginger. Press the slaw into a glass casserole dish, seal and refrigerate overnight to several days, stirring occasionally. The cabbage will turn a hot pink.

Before serving, garnish with toasted black sesame seeds and green scallion rings.

Cooking tip: The slaw stays delicious for a week or more.

Sweet Mama Squash Soup
Copyright The China Moon Cookbook

Preparation Time: 2 Hours
Pre-heat oven to 400°

    3 lbs. hard-skinned yellow squash, "Sweet Mama" our favorite
    3 Tbsps. fresh ginger, finely julienned
    ½ cup and 1 Tbsp. corn or peanut oil
    1 small yellow onion, sliced thin
    1 Tbsp. fresh ginger, finely minced
 1½ tsps. garlic, finely minced
    1 thumbnail-size piece cassia or cinnamon bark
    1 whole star anise, broken into 8 points
  10 cups unsalted chicken or vegetable stock
    Kosher salt, sugar and freshly ground pepper to taste
    ¼ cup almonds, sliced and toasted
    Fresh whole coriander leaves.

Cut squash in half, discard seeds and place cut-side down on a foil-lined baking sheet. Bake at 400° until very soft, about 50–60 minutes. Cool and discard peel. Cut squash into chunks.

Fry the julienned ginger threads until golden in oil and drain. Set aside.

In a large non-aluminum stockpot, heat 1 Tbsp. oil over moderate heat, adding the onions, ginger, garlic, cassia and star anise, tossing well to combine. Reduce the heat and cover the pot to "sweat" the onions until very soft and juicy, about 15 minutes. Add squash and stock, bringing soup to a near-boil, stirring occasionally. Discard cassia and anise and pureé soup in batches in a blender or food processor.

Before serving, bring the soup slowly to a near-boil over moderate heat. Adjust the tastes with kosher salt, sugar and pepper. Garnish with a hill of ginger threads, a sprinkling of almonds and a few strategically placed coriander leaves.

Cooking notes: Leftovers keep beautifully for 3–4 days, refrigerated.

Five-Spice Duck Breasts

Copyright The China Moon Cookbook

Preparation Time: 1 Hour (note refrigeration time)

   2 fresh whole duck breasts, skin left on
   1 Tbsp. five-spice powder
   1 tsp. dry mustard
   1 Tbsp. kosher salt
  ¼ cup rendered duck fat, corn or peanut oil
   Garnish of scallion threads, finely julienned

Cut the whole joined breasts in half along the keel line, trimming the individual breast pieces neatly at the borders. Remove any excess fat or cartilage.

Combine the five-spice, mustard and salt. Sprinkle evenly on both sides of the breasts, then rub well into the skin. Seal and set aside to marinate for several hours at room temperature or overnight in the refrigerator. Bring to room temperature before cooking.

In a large heavy skillet over high heat add enough duck fat or oil to glaze the pan. Reduce to medium heat and add the breasts, skin-side down in a single layer. Cook until the skin browns, about 3 minutes, then turn and brown the meat side 4 minutes more. The duck should be browned and the skin crispy on the outside, the meat medium-rare within. The fat will smoke during browning.

To serve, slice the breasts thinly, crosswise against the grain, and fan the slices at one end of the plate. Add a hill of cabbage slaw and garnish with scallion rings.

Cooking tip: This recipe serves 4 as a light entree or 6 as an appetizer. At China Moon Cafe, this dish is served with a citrus-dressed salad of baby greens and/or slices of sweet orange and persimmon.

China Moon Pickled Ginger

Copyright The China Moon Cookbook

Preparation Time: 25 Minutes
Yields: 2 Cups

½ lb. fresh ginger, peeled
1⅔ cup Japanese rice vinegar, unseasoned
½ cup plus 1 Tbsp. sugar
1 Tbsp. plus 1 tsp. kosher salt

Using a thin-bladed knife, cut the ginger crosswise against the grain into paper-thin slices.

Cover the ginger with boiling water, let steep 2 minutes, stirring once or twice, then drain.

In a non-aluminum saucepan bring the vinegar, sugar and salt to a boil, stirring to dissolve the sugar and salt. Pour over the ginger. Cool in a clean glass container and refrigerate.

Cooking tip: For best flavor, wait a day or two before using. Pickled ginger keeps indefinitely, refrigerated. However, the juice turns murky after several weeks.

Spicy Ginger Moons

Copyright The China Moon Cookbook

Preparation Time: 25 Minutes (note refrigeration time)
Pre-heat oven to 350°
Yields: 5–7 Dozen

 4 oz. unsalted butter, 1 stick
 ½ cup packed dark brown sugar
 1 Tbsp. fresh ginger, finely minced
 1 Tbsp. powdered ginger
 ½ tsp. vanilla
 1¼ cup all-purpose flour
 ¼ tsp. baking soda
   Pinch salt
 3 pieces crystallized ginger, cut into small pieces

Using an electric mixer and flat beater attachment, cream the butter and sugar on low speed until smooth. Add the fresh and powdered ginger, vanilla, flour, baking soda and salt. Continue mixing until the dough comes together.

On a large, flour-dusted piece of parchment paper, roll the dough to an even ⅛ in. thickness, dusting the roller as needed to prevent sticking. Slip the parchment onto a cookie sheet, then refrigerate the dough until firm, about 1 hour.

Slide the chilled dough on its parchment back onto the work table. Place a fresh piece of parchment on the cookie sheet. Using a moon-shaped or a round cutter, cut the dough and place on the lined baking sheet. Give each moon a decorative "eye" by pressing a sliver of crystallized ginger into the dough.

Bake on the middle rack of the oven until the cookie edges are lightly golden, 10–12 minutes. Remove to a rack to cool.

Cooking tip: Cookies keep nicely if sealed airtight up to a week, but flavor is keenest when freshly baked.

THE MANDARIN

CHINESE
900 North Point
Ghirardelli Square
673-8812
Open daily Noon–11PM
AVERAGE DINNER FOR TWO: $50

MADAME CECILIA CHIANG opened The Mandarin in 1968 and has recreated the atmosphere of dining in a cultured northern Chinese home. Softly-lit dining rooms with views of the bay blend the best of Chinese and San Francisco design. Silk-covered walls with ancient Chinese tapestry and beamed twig ceilings with natural wood pillars give the feeling of a home in the Forbidden City. Tables are set well apart to provide the luxury of conversational privacy.

Located in the Woolen Mill Building on the western edge of the square, facing onto North Point, The Mandarin offers excellent Peking-style cookery.

the mandarin

Chef Tzu Jia Yeh's Menu for Four

Hot and Sour Soup
Mandarin Minced Squab
Mongolian Lamb
Red-cooked Eggplant
Glazed Bananas

Hot and Sour Soup

Preparation Time: 25 Minutes

5 cups chicken broth
¼ lb. pork, cut into 1" julienne strips
¼ cup dried "Tree Ears" (mushrooms)
¼ cup bamboo shoots, sliced
1½ cakes fresh bean curd
1 Tbsp. dark soy sauce
1½ Tbsps. wine vinegar
¼ tsp. white pepper
1 egg, beaten
1 Tbsp. cornstarch
1 Tbsp. sesame oil
Garnish of 2 Tbsps. fresh coriander, chopped, optional

In a wok or large saucepan, bring the chicken broth to a boil and add the pork, mushrooms, bamboo shoots and bean curd for 10 minutes. Add soy sauce, vinegar and white pepper. Slowly add the beaten egg. Reduce to a simmer.

Dissolve the cornstarch in ½ cup cold water and stir into the soup. Sprinkle the sesame oil. Top with the coriander and serve.

Cooking tip: Do not add the egg too quickly or it will solidify into a single mass. The object is to have the egg form thin wispy flower-like shapes in the soup.

Mandarin Minced Squab

Preparation time: 45 Minutes

12 dried black mushrooms
2 large squabs, boned, chopped
1 cup water chestnuts, chopped
1 cup dried rice noodles
4 Tbsps. cooking oil
1 large tomato
2 scallions, chopped fine
2 tsps. ham, minced
1 Tbsp. rice wine or cooking sherry
1 Tbsp. oyster sauce
1 Tbsp. soy sauce
½ tsp. sesame seed oil
½ tsp. sugar
¼ tsp. white pepper
1 tsp. fresh ginger root, peeled, minced

Soak the black mushrooms in warm water for 20 minutes before chopping into fine pieces. Mix with squab and water chestnuts. Set aside.

Deep fry the rice noodles in warm (not hot) oil, then let cool. Crush noodles into medium sized pieces and spread on a serving platter.

Slice the tomato into wedges and place along the edge of the serving platter.

Heat cooking oil in a wok until hot. Add the squab and chopped scallions and stir-fry for 30 seconds. Add the rest of the ingredients and stir-fry another 2 minutes.

Serve the mixture in a rounded mound on the rice noodles.

Mongolian Lamb

Preparation Time: 15 Minutes

1½ lb. leg of lamb, boned
2 bunches scallions
3 Tbsps. oil
2 Tbsps. soy sauce
1 tsp. sesame oil
1 Tbsp. cornstarch mixed in 1 Tbsp. water

Cut the boned leg of lamb into thin slices. If you freeze the meat slightly, it will be easier to handle.

Shred the scallions lengthwise and cut into 2" segments.

Heat the oil in a wok on high heat and cook the lamb for 5 minutes. Add scallions, soy sauce and sesame oil. Toss well, then add the cornstarch solution to bind.

Remove from heat and serve.

Red-cooked Eggplant

Preparation Time: 25 Minutes

5 Chinese eggplants (banana-shaped)
¼ lb. lean pork
3 cups cooking oil
3 scallions, green part only
1 cup chicken stock
2 Tbsps. rice wine or cooking sherry
1 tsp. soy sauce
1 tsp. cornstarch mixed in 1 tsp. water
1 tsp. sesame oil
½ tsp. salt

Trim the stems off the eggplants and quarter lengthwise. Cut into 3″ sections. Heat the oil in a wok until very hot, and braise the eggplant for 1 minute. Remove the eggplant, and drain in a strainer. Remove all but 1 Tbsp. of oil from the wok.

Slice the pork into ½″ squares and stir-fry in the wok, until cooked through. Set aside.

Add remaining ingredients into the wok, for the sauce. When the sauce is hot, add the eggplant and pork. Stir-fry for 2 minutes.

Serve immediately.

Glazed Bananas

Preparation Time: 15 Minutes

3 semi-ripe bananas
½ cup all-purpose flour
2¼ cups cooking oil
1⅓ cup water
2 egg whites
1 cup sugar

Coat a serving platter with cooking oil.

Set aside a large bowl of ice water.

Cut each banana diagonally into 4 pieces. Dust each piece with flour. Shake off the excess.

Mix together ⅓ cup water, flour and egg whites for batter. When mixture is smooth, coat each banana with batter.

Heat the cooking oil in a wok or cast iron pan until medium hot. Deep fry the coated bananas until the batter turns golden brown, about 30 seconds. Set aside.

In another wok or pan, combine 1 cup water, sugar and ¼ cup oil for syrup mixture. Over high heat, stir constantly to prevent the syrup from burning. When the mixture begins to turn golden in color, add the banana pieces to the wok and coat them completely with the syrup.

Place the bananas onto the oil-coated plate and drop them into the ice water. Give the syrup about 5 seconds to crystallize and remove the bananas from the ice water.

Serve immediately.

TOMMY TOY'S

CHINESE
655 Montgomery Street
397-4888
Lunch Monday–Friday 11:30AM–3PM
Dinner daily 6PM–9:30PM
AVERAGE DINNER FOR TWO: $75

COMBINING THE REFINED atmosphere of French dining with the savory spices of Chinese cooking, Tommy Toy's has blended these two immortal cuisines into what Tommy calls "Frenchinoise." The result is classically elegant Chinese, yet contemporary French in style and taste. Tommy has carved his niche in a city whose culinary reputation is admired throughout the world.

While the cuisine is decidedly Chinese, the service is entirely French—at all times refined and courteous, yet personal and knowledgeable. The atmosphere is as elegant as the service, with the decor patterned after the reading room of the Empress Dowager of the Ching Dynasty. Diners are treated to a stunning visual display of elegance and splendor.

**HAUTE
CUISINE CHINOISE**

Chef Tommy Toy's Menu for Four

Black Mushrooms in Oyster Sauce
Lobster in Mango Cup
Chicken with Lemon Grass & Chile Pepper
Won Ton with Crab Meat & Chives
Vanilla Prawns

Black Mushrooms in Oyster Sauce

Preparation Time: 2½ Hours

8 oz. dried black mushrooms
1 green onion stalk
2 ginger pieces, sliced
6 oz. chicken meat, sliced
½ tsp. salt
1 tsp. sugar
3 oz. butter
1 cup chicken stock
   Splash of sesame oil
1½ Tbsp. soy sauce
1 Tbsp. oyster sauce
   Splash of white wine
1 tsp. cornstarch

Soak black mushrooms in water for 30 minutes.

Place green onion, ginger and chicken meat on top of whole mushrooms. Add salt and sugar. Put in a steamer and steam for 2 hours.

Remove and drain liquid. Discard chicken meat, green onion and ginger. Let mushrooms cool.

Melt butter in a pan. Add chicken stock, sesame oil, soy sauce, oyster sauce, wine, cornstarch and mushrooms.

Braise for 15 minutes on a low flame. The stock will boil away and concentrate the flavors in the mushrooms.

Serve plain.

Lobster in Mango Cup

Preparation Time: 2 Hours

2 ripe fresh mangoes
½ cup + 2 Tbsps. butter
2 cloves garlic, minced
½ lb. lobster meat, diced
¼ cup brandy
½ cup all-purpose flour
2 cups water
1 tsps. curry powder
2 tsps. purée of mango
½ cup pineapple juice
4 tsps. catsup
¼ cup white wine
¼ cup heavy cream
2 drops Tabasco sauce
½ tsp. salt
White pepper to taste

Cut mangoes in half the long way and remove seeds. Remove the mango meat in strips and set the mango cups aside.

Melt 2 Tbsps. butter in a heavy frying pan over medium heat and brown the garlic. Add lobster and sauté quickly for 30 seconds. Pour brandy over the lobster and flambé. Remove from heat and set aside.

Melt ½ cup butter in saucepan and slowly add the flour, stirring thoroughly until smooth. Slowly add the water and cook over low heat for 20 minutes until reduced to 1 cup. Add curry powder, purée of mango, pineapple juice, catsup, wine and cream. Stir and cook 2 minutes over low heat. Add Tabasco, salt, pepper and lobster, stirring for 1 minute.

Pour into mango cups and garnish with mango strips on top.

Chicken with Lemon Grass & Chile Pepper

Preparation Time: 45 Minutes

  6 garlic cloves, chopped
  1 stalk lemon grass, chopped
  2 chile peppers, chopped
  1 tsp. sesame oil
⅛ tsp. pepper
  1 tsp. sugar
  1 Tbsp. soy sauce
  2 Tbsps. white wine
  8 chicken breasts, skinless
  2 Tbsps. vegetable or olive oil
16 asparagus

Combine the first 8 ingredients for a marinade. Add chicken and marinate for 20 minutes.

Heat oil in a pan or wok at medium heat and cook the chicken, about 2 minutes on each side. Remove and drain.

Blanch asparagus in boiling water for 2 minutes. Remove and cook in pan or wok with a little oil and soy sauce for 30 seconds. Remove and drain.

On individual plates, place 2 pieces of chicken next to each other and 2 asparagus spears on each side of the chicken.

Won Ton with Crab Meat & Chives

Preparation Time: 15 Minutes

4 oz. crab meat
Small package cream cheese about 3 oz.
3 drops A-1 Sauce
½ tsp. salt
¼ cup chives, chopped
½ tsp. black pepper
¼ tsp. sesame oil
16 won ton skins
4 cups vegetable oil
Plum sauce for dipping

Mix the first 7 ingredients together in a bowl. Place ½ tsp. of the mixture on each corner of the won ton skin. Fold in half.

Heat oil in 350.° Deep fry until the won tons float and turn light brown, less than 1 minute.

Won tons can be served hot or cold. Dip in plum sauce.

Makes 4 per person.

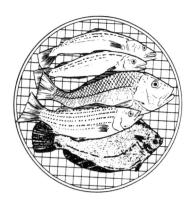

Vanilla Prawns

Preparation Time: 1½ Hours

1 Tbsp. sherry
⅛ tsp. sesame oil
¼ tsp. sugar
¼ tsp. white pepper
¼ tsp. salt
1½ tsp. corn starch in
   1 tsp. water

24 prawns
3 cups vegetable oil
8 won ton skins
1 Tbsp. paprika
Melon slices as garnish

Make a marinade of the first 6 ingredients.

Shell, devein and clean prawns in cold water. Drain and marinate for 20 minutes.

Heat vegetable oil to 500° in frying pan or wok. Add marinated prawns and cook for 30 seconds until lightly browned. Remove, drain and cool.

Add won ton skins to oil and cook until brown. Remove, drain and cool.

Mix prawns with vanilla sauce (see recipe below) and serve with fried won ton skins. Sprinkle with paprika and garnish with melon slices.

Vanilla Sauce

½ cup mayonnaise
¼ cup sweet condensed milk
1 tsp. raisins
1 celery stalk, chopped fine
1 tsp. vanilla extract
¼ tsp. ginger, chopped fine

Combine all ingredients to make vanilla sauce.

ACT IV

FRENCH
INN AT THE OPERA
333 Fulton Street
863-8400
Breakfast 6:30AM–10:30AM
Dinner and after theater 6PM–1AM
AVERAGE DINNER FOR TWO: $55

ACT IV RESTAURANT offers fireside dining in the luxury hotel, Inn at the Opera. The softly-lit dining room conveys old-world elegance amid beautiful oil paintings, leather dining chairs and plush velvet sofas. A flickering fire is reflected in the mirror above the polished wood bar. In the evening, a pianist plays classics and favorites on the grand piano.

The menu is innovative and trendy, offering Californian ingredients prepared in a French style. At the height of the performing arts season, Act IV offers theme menus such as the following opera recipe, "'Falstaff." This gracious meal is based on two Shakespearean plays, Henry IV and The Merry Wives of Windsor.

ACT IV

offering
Intimate fireside dining

Soft piano
accompaniment

Chef Greg Markey's Menu for Four

Rabbit Pie with Ginger Mustard
Filet of Sole with Sweet Onion Marmalade
Sherried Golden Chanterelles
Mixed Baby Beets
Chocolate & Vanilla Mousse with Amaretto Creme Anglaise

Ginger Mustard

Preparation Time: 15 Minutes (note ginger vinegar time)

½ cup brown mustard seed
2 Tbsps. ginger, minced
½ cup ginger vinegar
4 Tbsps. honey
2 shallots, minced
2 Tbsps. white wine
2 Tbsps. soy sauce

Place all ingredients in a blender and process until smooth. Add more wine to reduce thickness.

Cooking tip: Ginger vinegar can be made by adding 3 Tbsps. chopped ginger to a pint of cider vinegar. Steep at least 3 days.

Rabbit Pastry

Preparation Time: 20 Minutes (note marinating time)
Pre-heat oven to 375°

½ lb. rabbit meat
1 medium red onion, minced
½ cup celery, diced
½ cup carrot, diced
  Juice of 1 lemon
1½ cups port wine
4 Tbsps. olive oil
3 cloves garlic, minced
2 Tbsps. winter savory, chopped
2 Tbsps. chives, chopped
3 thyme sprigs
4 Tbsps. honey
1 sheet puff pastry
1 egg
  Pinch of salt and black pepper

Remove all fat and sinew from rabbit meat and dice in ½" square pieces.

Combine onion, celery, carrot, lemon, port, olive oil, garlic, savory, chives and thyme. Add rabbit and marinate in the refrigerator for 24 hours. Drain rabbit and mix in honey.

Cut pastry in 8 rounds. Place rabbit mixture in the center of 4 pastry rounds. Top the stuffed pastry with the remaining pastry rounds. Press edges with a fork to seal.

Make an egg wash by mixing 1 Tbsp. water with 1 egg. Brush the egg wash over the top of the pastry and bake at 375° for 20 minutes or until brown.

Serve warm with the spicy ginger mustard.

Filet of Sole with Sweet Onion Marmalade

Preparation Time: 15 Minutes

Four 8 oz. sole filets
1 cup flour
2 cups lemon juice
3 Tbsps. salt
3 Tbsps. black pepper
2 Tbsps. paprika
4 Tbsps. dill, chopped
Olive oil

Clean and wash filets and pat dry. Pour the lemon juice over the sole and set aside.

Mix flour with other dry ingredients and coat the sole in the herb flour mixture .

Sauté in olive oil until cooked.

Serve the sole with warm onion marmalade spooned on top.

Sweet Onion Marmalade

Preparation Time: 45 Minutes

¾ cup butter, unsalted
3 medium red onions, chopped
2 cloves garlic
3 scallions, chopped
2 Tbsps. salt
2 Tbsps. pepper

In a large saucepan, melt the butter on medium heat. Gently add the remaining ingredients. Cook 20 to 30 minutes or until very soft. Remove from heat and reserve ¼ cup.

Place the larger portion in a blender and process until very smooth.

Pour into a bowl and add the reserved steamed onion mixture. Stir well to blend.

Serve sole filets with the warm onion marmalade on top.

Sherried Golden Chanterelles

Preparation Time: 10 Minutes

½ **lb. Chanterelles, sliced**
4 **Tbsps. unsalted butter**
½ **cup dry sherry**
  Salt and white pepper to taste

Sauté the mushrooms in butter until brown. Add the sherry and reduce by half. Add salt and pepper to taste. Keep warm.
Serve with the sole filets and the sweet onion marmalade.

Mixed Baby Beets

Preparation Time: 45 Minutes

1 bunch red beets
1 bunch gold beets
6 Tbsps. butter, unsalted
¾ cup cognac
¾ cup brown sugar

Clean beets, leaving ¼" of top stem. Trim off bottom of root. Parboil each type of beet separately in salted water until cooked through. Rinse in cold water, peel and drain.

Sauté the beets in melted butter, but do not brown. Flambé with cognac. Add brown sugar slowly, until the sugar has melted and coated each beet.

Serve immediately.

Chocolate & Vanilla Mousse

Preparation Time: 25 Minutes (note refrigeration time)

¼ lb. semi-sweet chocolate
½ Tbsp. strong coffee
4 eggs, separated
½ Tbsp. brandy
1 Tbsp. vanilla

Melt the chocolate with coffee over water very slowly. Remove from heat. Add two yolks and brandy, mixing several minutes. Set aside.

Heat the remaining 2 egg yolks over water while whisking in the vanilla. Remove from heat and set aside.

Beat the 4 egg whites until stiff and fold half of the whites into the chocolate mixture and half into the vanilla mixture.

In a prepared mold or lined bread pan, pour both chocolate and vanilla mousse in alternating layers.

Chill 8 hours. Top with Amaretto creme anglaise.

Amaretto Creme Anglaise

4 egg yolks
½ cup sugar
1 cup milk
1 tsp. vanilla
2 Tbsps. Amaretto

Whisk yolks with sugar until pale. Set aside.

Heat milk in stainless steel pan until it begins to bubble. Slowly add the yolks, whisking continuously over low heat until thick.

Pour into a bowl to cool. Add Amaretto and refrigerate.

FLEUR DE LYS

FRENCH
777 Sutter Street
673-7779
Dinner Monday–Thursday 6PM–10PM
Friday–Saturday 6PM–10:30PM
AVERAGE DINNER FOR TWO: $95

FLEUR DE LYS RESTAURANT creates an elegant mood with a menu to match. This award-winning restaurant is noted for its true and simple contemporary French cuisine with a Mediterranean touch.

Chef-owner Hubert Keller believes in using only the best available produce, meats and seafood.

Fleur de Lys was designed by the late Michael Taylor. Using 700 yards of heavy fabric, hand-printed locally in a red floral pattern, Taylor created a feeling of an immense garden tent set in the French countryside. The mood is enhanced by strategically placed floor-to-ceiling mirrors. In the center of the room, under the peak of the tent, a towering arrangement of exotic flowers rises, highlighted by a Venetian chandelier above.

Fleur de Lys is a place for unhurried dining and quiet conversation in an intimate atmosphere.

Fleur De Lys
Restaurant Francais

Chef Hubert Keller's Menu for Four

Salmon in a Corn Pancake Topped with
Golden Caviar and Watercress Sauce
Chicken Breast Rolled Over Mushrooms & Spinach
with a Hazelnut Sauce
Creme Brulée & Caramelized Apples

Corn Pancakes

Preparation Time: 30 Minutes

6 oz. fresh Norwegian salmon
3 oz. golden caviar or sturgeon caviar
3 ears corn, cleaned
3 eggs
2 Tbsps. flour
Salt and pepper
2 Tbsps. cooking oil

Slice evenly and thinly 6 slices of salmon. On a plate, spread the salmon pieces with a tsp. of caviar. Fold in half so that the caviar is sealed between the two layers of salmon. Season with salt and pepper on both sides. Set aside.

Bring 4 quarts of salted water to a boil. Add the corn and boil for 5 minutes, then quickly dip in cold water. Cut the kernels from the cobs.

In a food processor combine the corn, eggs, flour, salt and pepper. Pour the batter into a small mixing bowl.

Grease a crepe pan or a frying pan with oil, heat. Add 1½ Tbsps. of the pancake mixture. Top the mixture with the slices of salmon and barely cover the salmon with another thin layer of corn mixture. Cook until golden brown on one side, turn and cook until golden brown on the other side.

Prepare the watercress sauce on the following page.

Watercress Sauce

Preparation Time: 25 Minutes

1 **bunch watercress**
½ **Tbsp. butter**
1 **Tbsp. shallots, chopped**
2 **Tbsps. dry white wine**
1 **Tbsp. chicken stock**
¾ **cup heavy cream**
18 **pieces asparagus tips, cooked**
4 **tsps. sour cream**
4 **tsps. caviar**
1 **Tbsp. chives, chopped**

Wash the watercress and trim off the leaves. Discard the stems. Cook the leaves in a pot of boiling salted water until tender, about 3 minutes. Drain in a strainer and refresh under cold water. Squeeze out any moisture in the watercress.

In a small saucepan heat butter and sauté the shallots until golden. Deglaze with white wine and reduce until almost dry. Add veal glaze or chicken stock and cream. Bring to a boil and reduce to a simmer. Add the cooked watercress leaves and blend well.

To serve, garnish pancakes with cooked asparagus tips. Top the pancakes with 1 tsp. of sour cream and 1 tsp. of caviar. Sprinkle with chopped chives.

Cooking tip: This dish has a pretty contrast of colors and a delightful taste which comes from the richness of the Norwegian salmon and caviar blended with the corn pancake and watercress sauce.

Stuffed Chicken Breast

Preparation Time: 15 Minutes

- 4 **large chicken breasts**
- 2 **bunches spinach leaves**
- 2 **Tbsps. butter**
- ¾ **cup wild mushroom (Chanterelles, Shiitake, Morels)**
- 2 **Tbsps. olive oil**
  - **Salt and pepper**

Stem the spinach completely. Carefully wash the leaves to remove all sand and grit. Place the washed leaves in a pre-heated sauté pan with butter, stirring occasionally until the leaves are wilted, about 3 minutes. Drain in a colander and squeeze out excess moisture.

Sauté the mushrooms in olive oil for 5 minutes. Add salt and pepper. Set aside.

Remove the skin and tendons from the chicken breasts and discard. Flatten each breast lightly with a large knife. Season the filets on both sides with salt and pepper. Top them with 1 Tbsp. of wild mushrooms and equal amount of wilted spinach. Roll each breast in 10" plastic wrap. Set aside.

Poach the chicken in the hazelnut sauce on the following page.

Hazelnut Sauce

Preparation Time: 1½ Hours

     Reserved chicken bones, chopped
 1 carrot, chopped
 1 onion, chopped
 1 celery stalk, chopped
 1 clove garlic, chopped
1½ cups white wine
 1 Tbsp. tomato paste
     Bouquet garni (bay leaf, thyme, parsley)
 4 cups water
 2 Tbsps. port wine
 4 Tbsps. butter
     Salt and pepper
 4 Tbsps. hazelnut oil

Roast the chopped chicken bones in the oven or sauté bones in a stock pot in oil. When bones are browned to a golden color, add the carrots, onions, celery and garlic. When the vegetables brown, remove any grease with a spoon and pour in the white wine. Add the tomato paste and the bouquet garni and reduce by half.

Add water and bring to a boil, skimming off any film that rises to the top. Lower the heat to a simmer and cook for 1 hour.

Pour the stock through a sieve. Discard the solids and skim off any fat.

Poach the chicken breasts in the plastic wrap for 12 minutes in the stock or until cooked. Remove the cooked chicken from the stock and keep warm.

Reduce the stock to ½ cup. Add the port wine and whisk in butter, a few pieces at a time. Stir in the salt and pepper to taste and add the hazelnut oil.

Remove the chicken breasts from the plastic wrap and slice the breasts on the bias. Serve with the hazelnut sauce.

Creme Brulée & Caramelized Apples with Orange Zest

Preparation Time: One hour

    3 cups cream
    1 orange for zest
 1½ lemons for zest
    9 egg yolks
  ¼ cup sugar
    3 Tbsps. butter
    2 apples, peeled, cut into 20 wedges
  ¼ cup brown sugar

Bring the cream with the orange and lemon zests to a boil.

In a mixing bowl, beat the egg yolks with the sugar. Continue whipping the egg mixture while pouring in the boiled cream. Set aside and let cool.

Prepare 4 oz. round molds and pour in the mixture of the creme brulée. Poach in a bain marie, so that the molds cook in the pan of water for 40 minutes.

In a large saucepan, sauté the butter and apples over high heat. Set aside and let cool.

When the creme brulée is poached, decorate the top of each with 5 slices of apples and sprinkle with golden brown sugar.

Broil the top of the creme brulée until the sugar melts and turns into a golden caramel color.

Serve warm or at room temperature.

FRENCH ROOM

FRENCH/CONTINENTAL
FOUR SEASONS CLIFT HOTEL
495 Geary Street
775-4700
Open daily 6:30AM—2:30PM
Dinner nightly 6PM—11PM
AVERAGE DINNER FOR TWO: $75

TRADITIONALLY, THIS HAS always been one of San Francisco's finest—a stately downtown hotel with high-ceilinged guest rooms and sophisticated Art Deco lounge. During the 1920s and '30s it was the exclusive spot for the exclusive set who met for haughty lunches in the hushed dining room. The Four Seasons Clift Hotel is as elegant today as it was back then, but without an ounce of snobbery.

The French Room now offers "Alternative Cuisine," offering dieters a delicious and satisfying alternative with low caloric and low sodium cooking. The discriminating dieter can choose from lobster consomme with Parisian vegetables, escalopine of veal with wild mushrooms or chicken with pearl onions, to name a few.

Chef Kelly Mills has provided us with the recipes for a Spanish Tapas dinner. The varied dishes, emphasize marinated foods that can be prepared in advance.

Four Seasons Clift Hotel
SAN FRANCISCO

Chef Kelly Mill's Menu for Four

Steamed Clams with Saffron & Pinenuts
Marinated Artichoke Salad
Pork & Eggplant Banderillas
Empanadillas filled with Rabbit & Olives
Orange Flan

Steamed Clams with Saffron & Pinenuts

Preparation Time: 15 Minutes

¼ cup olive oil
2 Tbsps. shallots, chopped
3 Tbsps. garlic, chopped
¼ cup spiced ham, diced into ¼" pieces
1 cup dry white wine
1 pinch saffron threads or powder
4 lbs. small steamer clams
1 cup tomatoes, diced
¼ cup dill, chopped
1 cup white bread crumbs, toasted
½ cup pinenuts, toasted
¼ cup parsley, chopped

Heat oil in a shallow casserole dish (large enough to steam clams). Sauté shallots, garlic and ham. Add white wine and saffron and bring to a boil. Add clams and cover, steaming until clams open. Remove clams and keep warm.

Add tomatoes and dill to broth. Whisk in the bread crumbs. Pour over clams in a serving bowl. Sprinkle with pinenuts and parsley.

Marinated Artichoke Salad

Preparation Time: 40 Minutes (note marinating time)

 1 Tbsp. coriander seeds
 2 bay leaves
10 peppercorns
 2 garlic cloves
 1 onion, diced into ½" pieces
 2 lbs. baby artichokes
 4 lemons, halved, juiced
 3 Tbsps. salt

Wrap the first 5 ingredients in cheesecloth to make a bouquet garni. Boil the artichokes with the bouquet garni, lemon juice and salt in 1 quart water until cooked, about 25 minutes. Remove from heat and cool.

Marinade

¼ cup chives, chopped
 1 cup onion rings
½ cup carrots, peeled, sliced
 2 Tbsps. walnut oil
½ cup salad oil
¼ cup sherry vinegar
¼ Tbsps. orange zest
 1 tsp. cayenne

Mix all ingredients and marinate artichokes overnight.

Pork & Eggplant Banderillas

Preparation Time: 25 Minutes

½ cup olive oil
2 lbs. pork butt, sliced
¼ cup onions, minced
¼ cup sugar
2 Tbsps. red wine vinegar
¼ cup sherry
1 cup brown sauce
¼ cup garlic puree
1 lb. eggplant, sliced into 1" cubes
2 tsps. paprika
¼ cup parsley

Heat ¼ cup olive oil in a skillet and sear the pork until brown on both sides. Remove the pork and add the onions. Sauté until golden. Add sugar and deglaze with vinegar and sherry. Bring to a simmer.

Add the brown sauce, garlic and meat, cooking until the meat is tender. Remove meat from the sauce and dice into 1" pieces.

In a separate skillet, heat ¼ cup olive oil and sear the eggplant until golden.

Skewer the pork and eggplant pieces and coat with sauce. Sprinkle with paprika and parsley.

Empanadillas Filled with Rabbit & Olives

Preparation Time: 2 Hours
Pre-heat oven to 350°

1 whole rabbit, cut up
3 Tbsps. olive oil
1 cup sweet onions, sliced
¼ cup fresh fennel, sliced
2 Tbsps. garlic, chopped
½ cup dry white wine
2 Tbsps. tomato paste
½ cup chicken stock
1 cup tomatoes, diced
1 9-oz. jar green olives,
   pitted, sliced

3 Tbsps. parsley, chopped
1 cup flour
1½ tsps. baking powder
½ tsp. salt
1 Tbsp. sugar
2 Tbsps. thyme
2 Tbsp. butter
½ cup milk
Egg wash (1 egg beaten
   with 1 Tbsp. water)

Heat olive oil in a skillet and brown the rabbit on all sides. Add onions, fennel and garlic and cook until onions shine. Add the wine and tomato paste and reduce by half. Add chicken stock, tomatoes and olives.

Simmer in a 350° oven for 1½ hours. If the liquid reduces too much, add more stock.

Cool the rabbit and pull all the meat off the bones. Dice into ½" chunks and add fresh parsley. Season with salt and pepper. Keep chilled.

In a large mixing bowl make the dough by combining flour, baking powder, salt, sugar, thyme and 1 Tbsp. parsley. Work butter and milk into the dough. Form into ball and let rest for 20 minutes.

Roll out dough ⅛" thick and cut 4‴ circles. Spoon rabbit mixture into the middle of each circle and fold over. Seal sides and top with egg wash. Bake at 450° until golden.

Orange Flan

Preparation Time: 45 Minutes
Pre-heat oven to 350°

¾ cup sugar
1 tsp. lemon juice
2 Tbsps. water
¾ cup milk
¾ cup cream
4 eggs
Zest from ½ orange
¼ cup Grand Marnier
Orange wedges
Whipped cream

In a heavy bottomed skillet, mix ½ cup sugar, lemon juice and water slowly until sugar starts to color. When golden brown, remove from heat and pour ¼" of the caramel ingredients into the bottom of 4 ramekins. Chill while preparing the custard.

In a saucepan combine the milk, cream, eggs, ¼ cup sugar, orange zest and Grand Marnier. Cook, stirring constantly, over medium heat until custard becomes thick.

Pour custard into the chilled ramekins. Place the ramekins in a pan filled with 1" of hot water and bake at 350° for 35 minutes.

Remove from oven and cool. Invert the molds onto a plate. Pour the remaining syrup over the custard and garnish with orange wedges and whipped cream.

THE SHERMAN HOUSE

FRENCH
2160 Green Street
563-3600

THE SHERMAN HOUSE is a sanctuary of time and space, a place where guests are bid welcome and invited to step into an ambiance governed by grace, beauty, and caring service.

Dining at The Sherman House is like being a privileged guest in the finest private home. The chef takes pride in preparing breakfast, lunch and dinner menus in the finest tradition of classical French Cuisine.

THE SHERMAN HOUSE

Chef Donia Bijan's Menu for Four

Cream of Winter Squash Soup
Cardamon Biscuits
Lobster with Sautérne Ginger Butter
Braised Rabbit with Cabbage Compote
Winter Fruits with Calvados Sabayon

Cream of Winter Squash Soup

Preparation Time: 45 Minutes

1 large butternut squash
1 yellow onion, diced
3 oz. butter
4 cups chicken broth
1 Tbsp. fresh ground cardamon
1 cup cream
   Salt and pepper to taste

Peel and remove seeds from squash and chop coarsely.

Sauté onions in butter until soft, add squash and stir together. Add chicken broth and cardamon, bring the soup to a boil. Reduce heat and allow to simmer until squash is cooked.

Pureé the soup in a blender and strain back into the pot. Add cream, salt and pepper. Bring to a boil and serve.

Cardamon Biscuits

Preparation Time: 20 Minutes
Pre-heat oven to 400°

½ **lb. all-purpose flour**
2 **oz. cold butter, sliced**
1 **tsp. salt**
2 **tsps. fresh ground cardamon**
   Zest of one orange
1 **cup cold cream**
   Egg wash (1 egg blended with 1 Tbsp. water)

Combine the flour, butter, salt and cardamon until crumbly. Add cream and orange zest, mixing gently. Do not overmix. Put the dough on a floured surface and pat it together to form a square 1″ in height.
Cut biscuits with a cookie cutter. Place on a baking sheet and brush with egg wash. Bake at 400° for 12 minutes until golden. Serve warm with the squash soup.

Soft Pillows of Lobster with Sautérne Ginger Butter

Preparation Time: One hour

½ lb. fresh lasagne dough
2 Maine lobsters, live
½ cup shallots, chopped
¼ cup ginger, chopped
1 cup sautérne or any sweet white wine
¼ cup lemon juice
¾ cup cream
3 oz. butter
1 cup carrots, steamed and julienned
Chervil sprigs for garnish

With a 5″ round cookie cutter cut 8 circles from the sheets of lasagne dough and cook in boiling salted water. Drain and refresh with ice water. Lay flat on greased cookie sheet. Cover with plastic wrap and set aside.

Cook lobsters in boiling water for 8 minutes. Remove and refresh in ice water. When cooled, remove from the shells and slice each lobster tail into 10 medallions. Each serving will have 5 pieces of tail and one claw. Refrigerate.

Sauté shallots and ginger in butter. Add wine and lemon juice. Reduce by half over low heat. Add cream and bring to a boil. Remove from heat and whisk in butter and season to taste. Strain and keep warm.

To assemble, warm the pasta in boiling water and place flat on the bottom of each plate. Warm carrots and lobsters in the ginger sauce and place on the pasta. Lay the second circle on top and place a lobster claw on top. Spoon more sauce over each and garnish with sprigs of chervil.

Braised Rabbit with Cabbage Compote

Preparation Time: 45 Minutes

2 fresh Sonoma rabbits
1 onion, sliced fine
1 head red cabbage, sliced fine
¼ cup red wine vinegar
2 Tbsps. sugar
1 Tbsp. fresh thyme, chopped
2½ cups apple juice
   Salt and pepper to taste

Have your butcher remove the loins and legs from your rabbit. If you have time, marinate your rabbit in virgin olive oil, rosemary, thyme and crushed garlic cloves for 24 hours. Make a stock with the bones.

Sauté the onions in butter until golden, add the cabbage, vinegar, sugar, thyme and apple juice. Bring to a boil, reduce heat and simmer for 30 minutes, stirring until the liquid has evaporated and the cabbage becomes soft. Season to taste.

Heat a sauté pan and braise the rabbit in virgin olive oil. Do not overcook or rabbit becomes very tough.

Remove the rabbit and add the remaining apple juice to the sauté pan. Bring to a boil. Strain and season to taste.

Serve rabbit over a bed of cabbage and spoon sauce over the top.

Cooking tip: Chopped apples or pecans are a delicious addition to the cabbage compote.

Winter Fruits
with a Calvados Sabayon

Preparation Time: 30 Minutes

  4 **egg yolks**
  ¼ **cup Calvados liqueur**
  ¼ **cup sugar**
  ¾ **cup cream, whipped**
  2 **cups ripe Comice pears, chopped**
  2 **cups Golden Delicious or Fuji apples, chopped**
  2 **tangerines, peeled and sectioned**
  1 **cup bananas, chopped**
  2 **Tbsps. powdered sugar**

To make the sabayon, whip the egg yolks, Calvados and sugar over a double boiler until thick and pale yellow, and doubled in volume. Remove from heat and cool.

Gently fold in whipped cream. Keep at room temperature.

Combine fruit and divide among four soup bowls. Pour sabayon over the fruits. Sprinkle with powdered sugar and place under the broiler until the tops become golden brown.

South Park Cafe

FRENCH
108 South Park
495-7275
Open Monday–Friday 8AM–10PM
Saturday 6PM–10PM
AVERAGE DINNER FOR TWO: $45

ENTERING SOUTH PARK is like stepping into the Left Bank of Paris. The picturesque oval park hidden in the middle of a city block is shaded by sycamore trees and sheltered from traffic.

The charming cafe that opens up onto the square has a terra-cotta floor and soft yellow walls. The butcher-papered tables and wall sconces with tiny silk shades, evoke the timeless quality of small neighborhood bistros in Paris.

Open all day during the week, you can start the day with croissants and cafe au lait. For lunch or dinner, enjoy classic cafe and bistro fare such as croque monsieur sandwiches filled with ham and gruyere cheese served hot, main course salads, steamed mussels, or stop by for wine and tapas.

Chef Benoit Dubuisson's Menu for Eight

Salade d'Avignon
Brie in Pastry with Calvados Beurre Blanc Sauce
Salmon in a Fennel Vinaigrette
Rabbit with Mustard
Lemon Tart

Salade d'Avignon

Preparation Time: 35 Minutes

2 Belgian endives
1 lb. mixed baby lettuce
1 lb. beets, cooked, peeled, diced
8 Tbsps. raisins
8 Tbsps. walnuts
1 apple, sliced into thin wedges

Place 4 leaves of endive on individual plates. Toss lettuce with vinaigrette and divide onto plates. Sprinkle beets, raisins and walnuts over salad. Garnish with apple slices.

Vinaigrette

2 Tbsps. lemon juice
2 Tbsps. balsamic vinegar
1 Tbsp. curry powder
½ Tbsp. garlic, chopped
¾ cup olive oil

Combine lemon juice, vinegar, curry and garlic in a food processor. Slowly add the olive oil while blending.

Brie in Pastry

Preparation Time: 25 Minutes
Pre-heat oven to 425°

   2 packages puff pastry
   1 egg yolk, beaten
   1 lb. brie cut into 8 cubes
   1 apple, peeled, cut into 16 wedges

     Cut puff pastry into sixteen 4" circles. Put 8 circles on a cookie sheet and brush edges with egg yolk. Put one piece of cheese and 2 apple slices on each and cover with remaining pastry circles. Brush top with egg yolk and score edges with a knife to seal.
     Bake 15 minutes or until golden brown.

Calvados Beurre Blanc Sauce

Preparation Time: 10 Minutes

   1 cup Calvados liqueur
   2 shallots, chopped fine
   ⅓ cup heavy cream
   ¾ lb. butter, soft
   Salt and pepper

     In a saucepan combine the Calvados with the shallots, reducing until almost dry. Add the cream and bring to a boil. Reduce heat and whisk in butter slowly. Do not allow to boil. Season with salt and pepper.
     To serve, pour sauce onto the serving plate and place brie in the center.

Salmon with Fennel Vinaigrette

1 bulb fennel
Juice of 2 lemons
3 cloves garlic, chopped fine
Salt and pepper to taste
3½ cups virgin olive oil
1 salmon filet from a 9 lb. salmon

Split and core the fennel and slice very thinly across the bulb. Set aside

In a bowl, mix the lemon juice, garlic, salt and pepper. Whisk in 2 cups olive oil and toss with fennel. Set aside.

Season the salmon (one whole side of the fish with the skin left on and all bones removed) with salt and pepper. Heat the remaining olive oil in a non-stick pan and place the salmon, skin side down, cooking over medium heat. Do not turn, the skin will prevent the fish from burning. When the middle of the filet is cooked and the top is rare the fish is done.

To serve, spoon the vinaigrette onto the center of the plate and place the salmon on it. Garnish with fennel.

Rabbit with Mustard

Preparation Time: 1½ Hours
Pre-heat oven to 325°

3 rabbits
1¼ cup Dijon mustard
   Pinch of rosemary
   Pinch of thyme
   Pinch of oregano
   Salt and pepper
3 cups heavy cream
2 cups dry white wine

Cut rabbits into 6 pieces each, 2 front legs, 2 rear legs, 2 saddles. Sprinkle with salt and pepper and place in an ovenproof baking pan in one layer.

Cover each piece with a coating of mustard and sprinkle evenly with herbs. Add cream and wine, which should come half way up the rabbit pieces. Cover pan with foil and bake for 1 hour or until meat is tender.

Remove rabbit and reduce sauce over medium heat until thick.

For each serving, place 2 pieces of rabbit on individual plate and pour the sauce over the rabbit.

Lemon Tart

Preparation Time: 45 Minutes
Pre-heat oven to 375°

2¼ cups flour
1¾ cups butter
 ¾ cup powdered sugar
 1 cup sugar
 8 egg yolks
 2 whole eggs
   Pinch of salt
10 lemons

In a stainless steel bowl make a well in the flour, put the powdered sugar, egg yolks, salt and 1⅓ cups butter in the middle. Mix well until dough forms into a ball. Refrigerate 30 minutes before forming dough into individual tart shells. Prick dough and bake at 375° for 15 minutes or until golden brown.

To make the lemon curd, zest the lemons and juice them to get 1 cup juice.

Melt ½ cup butter with the juice and sugar in a stainless double boiler. When melted, add whole eggs, stirring constantly until the mixture coats a spoon. Remove from heat and strain. Chill.

To serve, spoon filling into baked shells.

Stoyanof's Cafe & Restaurant

GREEK
1240 9th Avenue
664-3664
Lunch Tuesday–Sunday 10AM–5PM
Dinner Tuesday–Sunday 5PM–9:30PM
Friday & Saturday 5PM–10PM
AVERAGE DINNER FOR TWO: $30

THIS FAMILY OWNED and operated cafe is run by two generations of Macedonians who really know how to cook. Their food is consistently fresh, delicious and reasonably priced.

The menu features traditional Greek and Mediterranean specialties. All dishes, including desserts, are made in Stoyanof's kitchen.

The high-ceilinged contemporary dining room is gaily painted and well decorated with colorful flat woven rugs and Greek art work. Outdoor garden seating is available at umbrella-topped tables on the deck. Stoyanof's offers a warm, friendly, casual atmosphere, a good wine list and exceptional food.

Cafe and Restaurant by the Park

Chef Angel Stoyanof's Menu for Eight

Caciki (Cucumber Appetizer)
Spanakopita (Spinach & Cheese pastry)
Prawns with Feta
Roast Leg of Lamb
Sheker Paré (Turkish Cookies)

Caciki

Preparation Time: 15 Minutes (note yogurt draining time)

2 cups whole milk yogurt
1 medium cucumber, peeled, seeded
½ tsp. garlic, chopped
2 tsps. extra virgin olive oil
½ tsp. fresh dill, chopped
½ tsp. salt

Drain liquid out of yogurt by setting on a double thickness of cheesecloth. Drain for 3 hours.

Dice ¾ of the cucumber, mix with salt and set aside. Finely chop the remaining cucumber and put into a mixing bowl. Add the yogurt, diced cucumber, garlic, olive oil and dill. Mix well and refrigerate until ready to use.

Serve with pita bread.

Spanakopita

Preparation Time: 1½ Hours
Pre-heat oven to 350°

 1 small onion, finely chopped
 2 bunches fresh spinach, cleaned, dried
 1 egg
 3 Tbsps. cream
 ¼ lb. feta cheese, dried, crumbled
 2 Tbsps. extra virgin olive oil
 8 sheets filo dough
 ¼ cup melted butter

Sauté the onions in olive oil. Add spinach and cook until tender. Remove from heat and add remaining ingredients. Mix well. Refrigerate until ready to use.

Take 1 sheet filo dough, brush with melted butter and fold in half. Place 2 oz. or ⅛ of the spinach mixture in the front center of the filo sheet. Fold side edges of filo to center and roll up.

Place spanakopita on an oiled baking sheet and brush with butter. Bake for 30 minutes at 350° or until golden brown.

Cooking tip: These can be prepared ahead of time. Refrigerate until ready to bake.

Prawns with Feta

Preparation Time: One hour
Pre-heat oven to 400°

  2 tsps. garlic, chopped
  2 Tbsps. extra virgin olive oil
  ¼ cup white wine
  3 cups tomato sauce
32 prawns (about 2 lbs.), cleaned
  1 tsp. salt
  1 tsp. pepper
  8 tsps. fresh basil, chopped
  ½ lb. feta cheese, crumbled
    Parsley sprigs
    Lemon slices

In saucepan sauté garlic in olive oil until translucent. Add white wine, bring to a boil and simmer for 2 minutes. Add tomato sauce. Return to a boil and simmer uncovered for 15 minutes.

In a ceramic baking dish mix prawns with salt and pepper. Add tomato sauce, 4 tsps. basil and feta cheese.

Bake at 400° for 20 minutes. Remove from oven. Sprinkle with remaining basil and garnish with parsley sprigs and lemon slices.

Roast Leg of Lamb

Preparation Time: 20 Minutes (does not include cooking time)
Pre-heat oven to 350°

2 tsps. oregano
2 tsps. rosemary
1 Tbsp. salt
1 Tbsp. pepper
2 tsps. garlic, chopped
2 tsps. lemon juice
2 Tbsps. extra virgin olive oil
1 leg of lamb roast, boneless, rolled, tied
8 tomatoes, cut in wedges
2 tomatoes, puréed
2 bell peppers, chopped

In a small bowl, mix together oregano, rosemary, salt, pepper, garlic, lemon juice, and olive oil. Rub lamb roast with seasoning mixture. For better flavor this can be done a day ahead.

In bottom of roasting pan, mix together the cut and puréed tomatoes and the bell peppers. Set roast in pan and bake at 350° to desired doneness, (medium-rare is about 20 minutes per pound).

When done, remove roast from oven and let sit for 15 minutes. Save sauce from baking pan and skim off fat. Slice roast and serve with sauce.

Turkish Cookies

Preparation Time: One hour
Pre-heat oven to 350°

    4 cups flour
    ½ tsp. baking powder
    4 Tbsps. semolina
    3 Tbsps. almond paste
    ½ lb. butter, unsalted, softened
    4 medium eggs
36 almonds
    3 cups sugar
    1 qt. water

Sift together flour, baking powder and semolina. Crumble almond paste and add to flour mixture. Set aside.

Whip butter and fold in eggs.

Slowly add flour mixture into butter mixture until well mixed. Let sit for 15 minutes.

Divide dough into 36 equal parts and roll into balls. Press them gently onto greased cookie sheets and put an almond on top of each cookie. Bake at 350° for 30 minutes.

Put sugar and water in a saucepan and simmer until it is thick but not caramelized. Place cookies spaced tightly together in a single layer on a baking sheet with a lip. Pour the syrup over cookies while they are still hot and let sit for 3 hours.

Remove cookies from syrup to serve.

GAYLORD INDIA RESTAURANT

INDIAN
900 North Point
Ghirardelli Square
771-8822
Lunch daily Noon–1:45PM
Dinner daily 5PM–10:45PM
Sunday brunch Noon–2:45PM
AVERAGE DINNER FOR TWO: $45

GAYLORD'S IS RENOWNED around the world for its Tandoori specialties and true Indian hospitality. Tandoori cooking is a centuries-old North Indian technique using deep clay ovens. Meats, poultry and seafood are marinated for hours in special herbs and spices, then cooked quickly over hot charcoal. The result is a dish of marvelous flavor.

India's cuisine is a combination of subtle tastes. Flavors are as varied as India's climate. Fragrant, pungent spices from all over India are delicately blended to create Gaylord's special dishes. All of Gaylord's master chefs are from India and they have perfected the cuisine of their country.

Luxuriously decorated in pink linen with potted palms, Indian artifacts, soft music and candles, Gaylord's offers a relaxing and sensuous adventure.

**Simply
elegant dining.**

Chef Santokh Singh's Menu for Four

Dal Soup (Lentil Soup)
Lamb Shahi Korma
Tandoori Chicken
Rice Pillau
Kheer (Rice Pudding)

Dal Soup

Preparation Time: 45 Minutes

¼ lb. lentils
6 cups cold water
½ inch piece of ginger, chopped
2 garlic cloves, finely chopped
½ tsp. turmeric
½ tsp. cayenne
2 tsps. paprika
Salt to taste
½ cup heavy cream
Juice of one lemon

Wash lentils in standing water until water turns clear. Cook the lentils over high heat in 5 cups water. As water evaporates, add the sixth cup of water. Remove foam from the lentils with a slotted spoon and discard.

Add ginger, garlic, turmeric, cayenne, paprika and salt. Cook lentils until they turn mushy. Remove from heat and strain through a sieve.

Replace on low heat and add cream and lemon juice.

Serve immediately.

Lamb Shahi Korma

Preparation Time: 45 Minutes

  6 Tbsps. vegetable oil
  1 onion, sliced
  1 Tbsp. cumin seeds
  8 pods green cardamon, crushed
  2 sticks cinnamon
1½ lbs. lamb
  1 inch piece ginger, chopped
  4 garlic cloves, chopped
  ¾ cup plain yoghurt
  1 qt. milk
  1 tsp. turmeric
  1 tsp. cayenne pepper
  ¾ cup heavy cream
  ¼ cup sliced almonds
  ½ cup raw cashews
  2 Tbsps. fresh cilantro, chopped
  2 hard-boiled eggs, grated

Heat oil in skillet over medium heat adding onions, cumin seed, cardamon and cinnamon. Cook until onions are a light brown.

Cut lamb into ½″ cubes and add to onion mixture. Add the ginger, garlic, yoghurt, milk, turmeric, cayenne. Cook over high heat for 25 minutes, stirring constantly.

Lower heat and add cream, almonds. Grind the cashews to a paste and add to the lamb. Cover skillet and cook lamb until tender.

When cooked, garnish dish with cilantro and egg.

Tandoori Chicken

Preparation Time: 45 Minutes

    One 3 lb. chicken
6 cloves garlic
1 inch piece ginger root
1 cup plain yoghurt
    Juice of 1 lemon
1 tsp. salt
1 tsp. cayenne
1 Tbsp. paprika
1 tsp. cumin powder
    Melted butter
    Lemon wedges
    Raw onion

Skin, trim and disjoint the chicken into 4 pieces, discarding the wings and rib cage. Place 3 vertical slashes with a sharp knife into each piece of chicken. Set aside.

Make a marinade by grinding garlic and ginger in food processor. Add the yoghurt, lemon juice, salt, cayenne, paprika and cumin powder.

Marinate chicken overnight in a covered dish.

Pre-heat oven to the highest temperature and cook chicken for 10 minutes. After 10 minutes remove chicken and baste with melted butter. Reduce heat to 325° and cook chicken until done, about 20 minutes.

Garnish with lemon wedges and sliced raw onions.

Rice Pillau

Preparation Time: 45 Minutes
Pre-heat oven to 350°

    4 Tbsps. vegetable oil
    1 inch piece of fresh ginger, peeled, chopped
    1 clove garlic, chopped
    1 tsp. cumin seeds
    1 tsp. cinnamon
    3 pods of green cardamon, diced
    3 cups cold water
1½ cups Basmati rice
    Pinch of saffron
 ½ cup hot water
    Golden raisins
    Raw cashews

Heat oil in a pot and add the ginger, garlic, cumin, cinnamon and cardamon, browning for 5 minutes. Add 6 cups water and bring to a boil. Add rice.

Just before rice has finished cooking, add the saffron in hot water and mix well. Cover pot and place in a 350° oven for 10 minutes.

Garnish rice with golden raisins and raw cashews.

Kheer

Preparation Time: 45 Minutes

½ gal. milk
½ cup rice
1 Tbsp. raisins
3 Tbsps. sugar
1 Tbsp. almond slivers

In a heavy-bottomed pot, over high heat, bring milk to a boil. Stir constantly so milk will neither scorch nor overboil. When milk reaches the first boil, add the rice. When milk reaches the second boil, remove from heat for 1 minute without stirring. Replace on medium heat, stirring constantly.

When rice is cooked, about 30 minutes, add raisins, sugar and almonds to rice and remove from heat.

Serve the rice pudding either hot or cold.

CIAO

ITALIAN
230 Jackson Street
982-9500
Lunch and dinner Monday–Saturday 11AM–Midnight
Sunday 4PM–10:30PM
Full bar service
AVERAGE DINNER FOR TWO: $35

As YOU ENTER this energetic and popular trattoria, you will be treated to the aroma of fresh garlic and herbs. Venture through the doors to view the colorful variety of appealing antipastos on display.

The mood is uplifting in the multilevel dining room, enhanced by large windows and white ceramic tile floors. The bright white decor is accented by red flowers and the tail light of the Italian motor scooter on the wall. Braids of garlic and Italian sausages intertwined with streamers of fresh red, green and white fettuccine are hung to dry above the open kitchen.

The menu is innovative and intriguing, offering some of the fine regional cooking styles that have changed the Northern Italian dining scene. The homemade pastas combined with ingredients such as fresh artichokes, sundried tomatoes, radicchio and fresh shellfish create Italian delicacies that bring you to the streets of Milano.

Chef Luigi Negroni's Menu for Four

Radicchio alla Griglia (Marinated Grilled Radicchio)
Scamorza e Melanzane alla Griglia (Grilled Eggplant & Mozzarella)
Paglia e Fieno (Fettuccine, Pancetta, Peas, Cream)
Petti di Pollo Vincenzo (Stuffed Chicken Breasts in Wine Sauce)
Valentino (Chocolate with Raspberry Sauce)

Marinated Grilled Radicchio

Preparation Time: 15 Minutes

1 cup red wine vinegar
¼ cup extra virgin olive oil
2 cloves garlic, minced
  Salt and pepper to taste
2 large heads radicchio, quartered
  Lemon wedges for garnish

In a small bowl combine all ingredients except radicchio and lemon wedges, mixing thoroughly. Dip radicchio into mixture and grill over charcoal or on stove-top grill about 4 minutes, turning once.
Serve hot. Accompany with lemon wedges.

Grilled Eggplant & Mozzarella

Preparation Time: 20 Minutes

8 large eggplant slices, ⅓" thick
3 Tbsps. olive oil
  Salt and pepper to taste
3 oz. smoked mozzarella cheese, sliced ⅛" thick
  Fresh basil sprigs for garnish

Brush eggplant slices on both sides with olive oil. Place in single layer on baking sheet, season with salt and pepper. Broil until lightly browned and tender, turning once. Arrange eggplant, overlapping slightly in ovenproof serving platter. Top with cheese and broil just until cheese melts. Spoon sauce over eggplant. Garnish with basil. Serve immediately.

Lemon Herb Sauce

Yield: ½ cup

¼ cup olive oil
2 Tbsps. lemon juice
2 Tbsps. basil, chopped
2 Tbsps. parsley, chopped
  Salt and pepper to taste

In a small bowl, whisk together olive oil, lemon juice, basil and parsley. Mix in salt and pepper. Whisk just before serving.

Cooking tip: Eggplant and cheese can be arranged on individual ovenproof plates before melting cheese. Spoon 2 tablespoons sauce over each before serving.

Fettuccine, Pancetta & Cream

Preparation Time: 15 Minutes

1 lb. pancetta, cut into ¼" strips
1 cup butter
1 lb. fresh peas or thawed frozen peas
2 cups heavy cream
4 oz. each of egg fettucine and spinach fettucine
8 oz. Parmesan cheese, grated

In a large skillet, sauté pancetta until crispy. Drain and set aside. In a clean skillet, add the butter and melt over medium heat. Add peas and cook for 1 minute. Add cream and reduce slightly.

Meanwhile, cook pasta according to package directions and drain.

Add pasta, Parmesan and pancetta to cream mixture. Toss to combine. Serve hot.

Cooking tip: Eight oz. prosciutto may be substituted. Do not cook prosciutto but add to the skillet with the peas.

Stuffed Chicken in Wine Sauce

Preparation Time: 30 Minutes

16 mint leaves
16 sage leaves
 4 Tbsps. rosemary leaves
1½ tsps. anise seeds
 3 Tbsps. olive oil
 2 tsps. pepper
1½ tsps. salt
 4 boneless chicken breast halves, with skin
12 marinated sundried tomato halves, drained
 2 oz. Fontina cheese, thinly sliced
 2 Tbsps. butter
 1 small onion, chopped
 ½ cup white wine
 ¼ cup lemon juice
 ¼ cup parsley, chopped

In a food processor blend the mint, sage, rosemary and anise 15 seconds. Add oil and 1 teaspoon each of the pepper and salt. Process 15 seconds.

Make pockets under the chicken skin and stuff with herb mixture, tomatoes and cheese, dividing equally.

Heat butter over medium heat in a large skillet, adding the chicken, skin side down. Cook 10–12 minutes, turning once, until juices run clear. Remove from skillet and keep warm.

Add the onion to the skillet and sauté for 1 minute. Add wine, lemon juice, parsley and remaining 1 teaspoon pepper and ½ teaspoon salt. Reduce slightly.

Serve sauce over chicken.

Chocolate with Raspberry Sauce

Preparation Time: 30 Minutes (note refrigeration time)

1 ½ cups unsalted butter, softened
9 hard-cooked egg yolks
12 oz. semisweet chocolate, melted and slightly cooled
¾ cup prepared fudge topping
½ cup unsweetened cocoa powder
3 Tbsps. brandy
2 Tbsps. Amaretto liqueur
1 Tbsp. vanilla extract
6 oz. semisweet chocolate, shaved or finely chopped
4 oz. Amaretti cookies
½ cup cooled espresso coffee
36 oz. unsweetened frozen raspberries, thawed
6 Tbsps. sugar
Mint sprigs and Amaretti cookies for garnish

Cream the butter in a large mixing bowl. Force yolks through a fine sieve into butter. Beat until smooth. Add melted chocolate, fudge topping, cocoa, brandy, Amaretto and vanilla. Beat at medium speed until light and fluffy, 8 to 10 minutes. Mix in shaved chocolate.

Oil a 9 × 5″ loaf pan and line smoothly with plastic wrap. Spread ⅓ of the chocolate mixture in bottom of pan.

Dip half the cookies, one at a time, into coffee and arrange evenly on chocolate layer. Cover with half the remaining chocolate mixture. Smooth top and repeat with remaining cookies. Smooth top and press down firmly to eliminate air spaces.

Cover and refrigerate several hours or overnight.

In a blender puree the raspberries. Force through a fine sieve. Mix in sugar to taste.

To serve, spoon 3 Tbsps. raspberry puree onto each plate and top with slice of chocolate loaf. Garnish with mint sprigs and crushed Amaretti cookies.

Cooking tip: Slice with a sharp knife dipped into hot water.

DONATELLO

ITALIAN
DONATELLO HOTEL
501 Post Street
441-7100
Breakfast 7AM–10:30AM
Dinner 6PM–11PM
AVERAGE DINNER FOR TWO: $100

SINCE OPENING IN 1980, Ristorante Donatello has been recognized as one of San Francisco's finest Italian restaurants. Its reputation for excellence has been earned by combining the best of Italy and California in a romantic, intimate dining atmosphere. The unique menu offers a fresh interpretation of Northern Italian cuisine.

Located in the Mobil-Four Star Donatello Hotel, this award-winning restaurant is resplendent in Italian marble and fine appointments, promising an elegant dining experience. The Donatello offers an outstanding wine list, decadent desserts and a weekly "prix-fixe" menu, featuring the chef's personal recommendations.

THE DONATELLO

Five Hundred & One Post Street
San Francisco, California 94102

Chef Luigi Mavica's Menu for Six

Baby Beet & Bean Salad
Pasta Tubes with Pheasant Ragout
Halibut Encrusted with Potato & Rosemary
Stuffed Lamb in Black Olive Sauce
Risotto Tambales

Baby Beet & Bean Salad

Preparation Time: 30 Minutes.

3 bunches baby golden or red beets
6 Tbsps. balsamic vinegar
¼ cup virgin olive oil
   Salt and white pepper
½ cup green beans, 2" long
1 sweet onion, peeled, quartered
3 heads romaine or oak leaf lettuce
6 sprigs Italian parsley

Trim the stems and roots from the beets and cook beets in lightly salted water for 15 minutes or until tender. Rinse in cold water, drain, peel and quarter the beets. In a bowl, toss the beets with 2 Tbsps. balsamic vinegar, 4 Tbsps. olive oil, salt and pepper. Set aside.

Cook the green beans in boiling salted water for 2 minutes, or until tender. Rinse in cold water and drain. Toss the beans separately with 2 Tbsps. balsamic vinegar, 4 Tbsps. olive oil, salt and pepper. Set aside.

To assemble the salad, place leaves of lettuce on chilled salad plates radiating from the center of the plate. Place small bundles of green beans between each lettuce leaf. At the last moment, toss the beets with the onion slices and parsley, then mound the beet mixture in the center of the plate. Drizzle 1 tsp. of olive oil and ½ tsp. balsamic vinegar over the lettuce leaves.

Pasta Tubes with Pheasant Ragout

Preparation Time: 2 Hours

1 pheasant, about 2 lbs.
1 onion, diced
1 stalk celery, diced
1 carrot, diced
3 Tbsps. basil, chopped
1 Tbsp. rosemary, chopped
1 cup red wine
1 29 oz. can whole peeled tomatoes
1 Tbsp. tomato paste
   Garganelli pasta tubes
   Parmesan cheese, grated

Bone the pheasant, removing the skin from the breasts and legs. Mince the meat using a large chef's knife. Put the meat, diced vegetables and chopped herbs into a heavy pot and cook over medium heat, until the meat is lightly brown, about 5 minutes. Pour in the wine and continue cooking until it is reduced by half.

Remove any seeds from the tomatoes, then roughly chop them. When the wine has reduced, add the tomatoes to the pot, along with their juice and the tomato paste. When the ragout has come to a boil, simmer uncovered for 1½ hours, skimming any fat from the surface. Should the ragout become too dry before the end of the cooking time, add a little water to adjust the consistency. Season with salt and freshly ground black pepper.

Cook the garganelli pasta in salted boiling water. The time will depend on whether the pasta is fresh, (as little as one minute), or dry, (7–8 minutes). When the pasta is cooked, add it to the ragout, mix well and spoon into a serving dish. Pass freshly grated Parmesan cheese on the side.

Halibut Encrusted with Potato & Rosemary

Preparation Time: 30 Minutes
Pre-heat oven to 450°

2½ lbs. halibut filets
  2 russet potatoes
  2 sprigs rosemary, chopped
12 oz. virgin olive oil
    Salt and pepper

Trim the halibut filet and cut into 6 oz. portions.

Slice the potatoes into translucently thin slices. Wash the potato slices twice and keep in water until ready to use.

Lightly coat the bottom of an ovenproof baking dish with olive oil. Season the halibut and place in the dish, being careful not to crowd the filets. Cover each portion of halibut with potato slices, slightly overlapping each slice. Sprinkle the rosemary on top of the potato slices. Pour the wine into the baking dish and place in the oven for 15 minutes or until the potatoes are tender.

Place each filet on warm serving plates and pour 1½ to 2 oz. of olive oil over the filets.

Loin of Lamb Stuffed with Caponata in Black Olive Sauce

Preparation Time: 2 Hours
Pre-heat oven to 400°

  1 green zucchini, diced
  1 yellow zucchini, diced
  1 red bell pepper, diced
  1 yellow bell pepper, diced
  2 Japanese eggplants, diced
  3 cloves garlic, minced
½ cup pine nuts, toasted
   Virgin olive oil
   Salt and black pepper
  1 saddle of lamb

Combine the green and yellow zucchini together and set aside. Combine the red and yellow bell pepper together and set aside.

Heat a heavy skillet over high heat and sauté the eggplant in the olive oil with ⅓ of the garlic, salt and pepper until cooked, about 3 minutes. Put the eggplant into a colander to drain the excess liquid. Repeat this process with the zucchini and bell pepper, adding each to the eggplant in the colander. When all the vegetables have been sautéed, add the toasted pine nuts and mix the caponata together. Put the cooled caponata into a pastry bag.

Bone the saddle of lamb and cut a pocket in each loin. Pipe the caponata into the pocket. When the pocket is filled, secure the open end with a wooden toothpick or short skewer.

Heat a large ovenproof skillet until hot. Season the lamb loins and brown on each side about 2 minutes. Put the loins in the pre-heated oven to cook for 10 minutes. The meat should be pink and the caponata just warmed through.

Slice each loin across into thin slices and spoon the sauce (recipe follows) around the lamb, and serve.

Black Olive Sauce

Lamb saddle bone,
  chopped
Meat scraps from
  the saddle
4 shallots, chopped
2 garlic cloves, chopped
2 sprigs fresh thyme

6 black peppercorns
2 bay leaves
1 small jar nicoise olives
2 cups Madeira wine
1 qt. lamb or veal stock
2 Tbsps. cornstarch

Pit and cut the olives in half, drain and set aside for garnish, reserve the brine.

Roast the lamb bones and meat scraps 40 minutes or until browned over medium heat. Reduce heat, remove the bones and add the shallots, garlic, herbs, olives and deglaze with the wine. Reduce by ⅔ and add the stock and bones. Bring the sauce to a simmer, skim well and set to cook for 1 hour.

Adjust the sauce if necessary by adding a little of the olive brine. Dissolve the cornstarch in 2 Tbsps. water and add enough to thicken the sauce. Strain through a fine mesh strainer.

Risotto Tambales

2 cups arborio rice (risotto)
2 Tbsps. butter
¼ cup Parmesan cheese
  Olive oil

Cook the rice according to package directions. When cooked, add butter and Parmesan.

Coat six 8 oz. custard cups with olive oil and fill each half full with the hot risotto. Cool and refrigerate until ready to use.

Unmold the cold risotto tambales and place bottom side down into a buttered skillet. Cover and cook in the oven for 10 minutes at 350°. When the risotto is heated through and the bottom surface is golden brown, serve with the lamb and black olive sauce.

KULETO'S

ITALIAN
221 Powell Street
397-7720
Breakfast, lunch and dinner daily 7AM–11PM
Bar open until midnight
AVERAGE DINNER FOR TWO: $40–$50

THE ATMOSPHERE OF Kuleto's is a combination of old San Francisco with contemporary vitality. High-vaulted ceilings and Italian marble floors are complemented by dark woods and warm lighting. Garlands of garlic, dried peppers, sausages and herbs hang over a magnificent mahogany bar, where tempting antipasto dishes are displayed. The 40-foot-long Brunswick bar represents pure history; it was made in England and brought 'round Cape Horn by sailing ship before the turn of the century.

The menu is distinctive California-Italian cuisine featuring fresh ingredients prepared in unusual combinations. Highlights include original pastas, innovative salads, grilled fresh fish and roasted meats and poultry. The baked goods, breads and desserts are made fresh daily on the premises.

KULETO'S

Italian Restaurant

Chef Robert Helstrom's Menu for Four

Baked Chevre with Sundried Tomatoes and Basil
Tomato, Sausage & Foccacia Soup
Fettucine con Funghi (Mushroom Fettucine)
Petto di Pollo with Roasted Pepper Sauce (Chicken)

Baked Chevre with Sundried Tomatoes and Basil

Preparation Time: 30 Minutes
Pre-heat oven to 450°

Olive oil
8 oz. log of goat cheese
4 oz. sundried tomatoes in oil, chopped
½ tsps. garlic, chopped
½ cup fresh basil leaves, chopped
Crackers

Oil a small baking dish lightly with olive oil. Place a log of cheese in dish and bake for 25 minutes.

Mix together the sundried tomatoes, garlic and basil. Top cheese with this mixture and serve with crackers.

Tomato, Sausage and Foccacia Soup

Preparation Time: 25 Minutes

1 onion, diced small
2 cups celery, diced small
2 Tbsps. garlic, chopped
½ gal. whole pear tomatoes
2 hot Italian sausages, sliced
1 tsp. fennel seed
1 tsp. red chiles, crushed
Salt and pepper to taste
1 Tbsp. lemon juice
Foccacia bread, cubed
Extra virgin olive oil
Parmesan cheese

Sauté the onions and celery in olive oil. Add garlic and tomatoes and purée the stock. Let simmer.

Blanch sausages in stock. Remove and let cool.

Season stock with fennel seed, red chiles, salt, pepper and lemon juice. Whisk foccacia into soup.

Place sausages in serving bowl and ladle soup into bowl. Garnish with olive oil and Parmesan cheese.

Mushroom Fettuccine

Preparation Time: 20 Minutes

1 Tbsp. shallots
2 garlic cloves, chopped
  Olive oil
1 qt. veal stock
1 qt. Maderia wine
¼ cup oyster mushrooms, chopped
¼ cup shiitake mushrooms, chopped
½ cup morel mushrooms, chopped
4 Tbsps. butter
1 lb. black pepper fettucine, cooked
1 Tbsp. sage, chopped
  Salt and pepper to taste

Sauté shallots and garlic in olive oil. Add veal stock, Madeira wine and mushrooms.

Add butter, fettucine and finish with sage, salt and pepper to taste. Serve immediately.

Chicken with Roasted Pepper Sauce

Preparation Time: 45 Minutes
Pre-heat oven to 425°

   4 chicken breasts, wing bone attached
1½ cups ricotta cheese
   2 Tbsps. sundried tomatoes, chopped
  ¼ cup fresh basil, chopped
   3 Tbsps. fresh oregano, chopped
   2 Tbsps. fresh chives, chopped
   3 Tbsps. olive oil
   1 Tbsp. garlic, minced
  ½ cup dry white wine
   1 red bell pepper, roasted, peeled, julienned
   1 yellow bell pepper, roasted, peeled, julienned
   6 Tbsps. unsalted butter

In a mixing bowl, combine ricotta, tomatoes, basil, oregano and 1 teaspoon chives. Season to taste. Fill a pastry bag with the stuffing mixture.

Make a slit in the side of each breast and cut a pocket from one end to the other. Insert ¼ of the stuffing mixture into each breast. Dust the chicken with flour.

Heat the olive oil in a sauté pan and brown the chicken. Remove to a baking dish and bake for 15 minutes or until the flesh between the bones and breast turns white.

Pour off any excess oil from the sauté pan and sauté the garlic briefly over medium heat. Deglaze with white wine. Turn the heat up to high and reduce by half. Add the peppers and whisk in the butter. Remove from heat. Add 1 tsp. chives and season to taste.

Razing the walls of the old Palace Hotel, one of the most spectacular photographs taken during the rebuilding of San Francisco. These walls were pulled down with wire cables operated by donkey engine.

LA FIAMMETTA

ITALIAN
1701 Octavia at Bush
474-5077
Dinner daily 6PM–10PM
AVERAGE DINNER FOR TWO: $45

LIKE THE ROMAN restaurant for which it is named, La Fiammetta offers excellent food in an unpretentious setting, with Italian-style hospitality. The staff strives to make you feel like a neighbor, whether you are a local or a visitor to San Francisco.

Chef Paul Cattoche and partner Jack Krietzman have created a menu based on authentic Roman and Tuscan tastes. The wine list features a good selection of Italian and California wines.

La Fiammetta is a cozy, upscale haven where hearty conversation, great food and wine and expert service prevail. A secret place that local residents and business executives would prefer to keep to themselves.

Buon appetito.

Chef Paul Cattoche's Menu for Four

Grilled Radicchio
Eggplant & Arugula Salad
Risotto Bianco
Filet Mignon with White Truffles
Raspberry Walnut Tart

Grilled Radicchio

Preparation Time: 30 Minutes

2 heads radicchio
4 oz. Fontina cheese
8 oz. pancetta (Italian bacon)
½ cup balsamic vinegar
½ cup fresh basil, chopped
¼ tsp. ground black pepper
1 cup virgin olive oil

Cut radicchio into 6 wedges. Take each wedge and insert a sliver of cheese. Then wrap pancetta around the radicchio.

Make a sauce by combining the vinegar, basil, pepper and olive oil. Set aside.

Grill the radicchio until dark brown. Pour sauce over the radicchio and serve warm.

Eggplant & Arugula Salad

Preparation Time: 45 Minutes
Pre-heat oven to 350°

1 medium eggplant
1½ cups virgin olive oil
1 tsp. red wine vinegar
½ cup arugula leaves
1 red bell pepper
4 cloves garlic

Slice eggplant in ¼″ slices and dip in a bowl of 1 cup olive oil with the vinegar. Grill the eggplant until dark. Remove from heat and cut the eggplant into bite-sized pieces. Mix the eggplant with the arugula leaves.

Cut bell pepper into 4 sections and place on a baking sheet. Put 1 clove of garlic in each section and drizzle with olive oil.

Roast in the oven until the bell pepper skin is black and the garlic dark brown. Peel bell pepper and chop fine with garlic. Add ½ cup olive oil to the bell pepper garlic mixture.

Add the bell pepper garlic mixture to the eggplant. Drizzle with additional olive oil if desired.

Risotto Bianco

Preparation Time: 45 Minutes
Pre-heat oven to 450°

  1 cup arborio rice (risotto)
1½ cups chicken broth
1½ cups dry white wine
  1 Tbsp. celery, finely chopped
  1 tsp. garlic, finely chopped
  1 sprig fresh thyme
  2 Tbsps. butter
    Salt and white pepper to taste
12 medium prawns, peeled, deveined
  8 large scallops

In a large sauté pan add rice, broth, wine, celery, garlic, thyme, and half the butter. Bring mixture to a boil, stirring frequently. Remove from heat and place in a 450° oven for 5–7 minutes, uncovered.

Remove from oven and add remaining ingredients, bringing rice to a boil over high heat, again.

Put rice back in the oven uncovered, for 5–7 minutes. Serve immediately.

Filet Mignon with White Truffles

Preparation Time: 10 Minutes

1¼ lb. center cut filet mignon
¼ cup white truffles, shaved or sliced thin
2 Tbsps. extra virgin olive oil

Slice the filet mignon into 8 medallions, approximately 2½ oz. each.

Grill the filet to desired doneness and smother with the raw white truffles.

Drizzle ½ tsp. extra virgin olive oil on each filet.

Serve immediately.

Raspberry Walnut Tart

Preparation Time: 30 Minutes
Pre-heat oven to 400°

½ cup butter
1 cup sugar
1 tsp. vanilla extract
2 cups + 1 Tbsp. flour
1 cup walnuts
2 eggs
2 baskets of raspberries

In a food processor mix ¼ cup butter, ½ cup sugar and the vanilla extract until creamy. Slowly add 2 cups flour. Stir pastry only until mixed.

Spread the pastry in a pie plate and prick the bottom with a fork. Bake the crust for 20–30 minutes in 400° oven until brown. Take out and let cool slightly.

Make the walnut cream by combining the walnuts, eggs, ¼ cup butter and ½ cup sugar in a food processor. Add 1 Tbsp. flour and blend until smooth.

Put raspberries in the pie crust and pour the walnut cream over the raspberries

Bake for 20–25 minutes in 350° oven.

PREGO RISTORANTE

ITALIAN
2000 Union Street at Buchanan
563-3305
Lunch and dinner daily 11:30 AM–Midnight
Full bar service
AVERAGE DINNER FOR TWO: $40

WITHOUT A DOUBT, Prego is one of the locals' most popular restaurants—and with good reason.

Specializing in Northern Italian cuisine, Prego presents dishes that are fresh and simply prepared—and with a great deal of imagination. Authentic Italian pizza is baked in an oak-burning brick oven. Homemade pasta, charcoal-grilled fresh fish and spit-roasted meats and fowl round out the menu.

Prego offers an extensive list of wines from Italy and California in addition to a full bar.

The atmosphere is warm and friendly in this lively Union Street trattoria. Look up to the skylight when open, it reveals an herb garden on the roof.

Chef Bobby Estenzo's Menu for Six

Gamberetti Marinati (Shrimp, Feta Cheese in Vinaigrette)
Fagioli con Tonno (Tuna with White Beans & Radicchio)
Conchiglie al Carciofo e Spinaci (Pasta, Artichokes, Spinach,
Pancetta in Cream)
Osso Buco con Polenta (Veal Shanks, Tomato Sauce & Polenta)
Tiramisú (Espresso-soaked ladyfingers, Mascarpone Cheese & Rum)

Shrimp & Feta Cheese

Preparation Time: 1½ Hours

⅓ cup extra virgin olive oil
3 Tbsps. fresh mint,
    chopped
½ tsp. salt
½ tsp. pepper

1 lb. medium prawns,
    peeled and deveined
Lime halves and mint
    sprigs for garnish

Combine all ingredients for marinade. Add prawns and marinate for ½ hour. Remove prawns from marinade and grill or broil about 1 minute, turning once, until opaque. Cool slightly and refrigerate ½ hour.

Vinaigrette

⅓ cup extra virgin olive oil
Juice of 2 to 3 limes
3 Tbsps. feta cheese,
    crumbled

3 Tbsps. fresh mint,
    chopped
1½ tsps. salt
1½ tsps. pepper

Combine all ingredients for vinaigrette. Toss with prawns and let stand 15 minutes. Arrange on plates and garnish prawns with lime halves and mint sprigs.

Tuna with White Beans & Radicchio

Preparation Time: 15 Minutes (note refrigeration time)

2 lbs. white beans, cooked
¾ lb. albacore tuna, grilled and chopped
¾ cup white onion, chopped
½ cup lemon juice
6 Tbsps. extra virgin olive oil
Salt and pepper to taste
2 cups radicchio, coarsely chopped
Chopped basil for garnish

In a medium bowl combine beans, tuna, onion, lemon juice and oil, tossing thoroughly. Season with salt and pepper.

Cover and refrigerate 1 to 4 hours. Bring to room temperature.

Add radicchio and toss well. Sprinkle with basil. Drizzle with additional oil if desired.

Pasta, Artichokes, Pancetta in Cream

Preparation Time: 1½ Hours

12 baby artichokes, washed
½ cup dry white wine
   Juice of 1 lemon
3 oz. pancetta, cut into ⅓" cubes
2 cups heavy cream
6 Tbsps. butter
1 lb. medium conchiglie (dry pasta shells)
3 tsps. salt
1 tsp. pepper
4 cups spinach leaves, cut into ½" strips
3 egg yolks, beaten
¾ cup Parmesan cheese, grated
2 Tbsps. parsley, chopped

In a 3 quart saucepan combine artichokes, wine, lemon juice, 1 teaspoon salt and enough water to cover. Cook until tender, about 20 minutes. Drain and peel off outer leaves. Quarter the tender hearts and set aside.

Sauté the pancetta over medium heat until browned, about 5 minutes. Drain and set aside. Discard fat.

In same saucepan combine cream and butter, cooking over medium heat about 10 minutes until reduce by ¼.

Meanwhile, cook pasta in 1 gallon boiling water with the salt.

Mix the artichokes, pancetta and pepper into the cream mixture. Keep warm.

When pasta is al dente, add spinach and continue to cook 1 minute. Pour into colander and drain thoroughly. Return pasta and spinach to pot. Add cream mixture, tossing gently over medium heat about 2 minutes until hot. Remove from heat. Gently mix in yolks and half the cheese.

Transfer to platter, dust with remaining cheese and sprinkle with parsley. Serve immediately.

Cooking tip: One package (9 oz.) frozen artichoke hearts, thawed, drained and quartered can be substituted.

Veal Shanks in Tomato Sauce

Preparation Time: 3 Hours

2 Tbsps. olive oil
6 medium-sized veal
   shanks (about 4 lbs.)
1 large onion, chopped
2 cloves garlic, minced
2 carrots, peeled and diced
2 celery stalks, diced
1 dozen Roma tomatoes,
   cut into ½" chunks

1½ cups veal or chicken stock
1 cup dry white wine
3 Tbsps. fresh rosemary,
   chopped
4 bay leaves
1 tsp. salt
1 tsp. pepper
2 Tbsps. water
1 Tbsp. cornstarch

Heat oil over medium-high heat in Dutch oven or oven-proof pan. Add veal and brown, turning once. Remove veal and set aside. Add onion and garlic, sauté 1 minute. Add carrots and celery, sauté 2 minutes.

Return veal to pan, adding tomatoes, stock, wine, rosemary, bay leaves, salt and pepper. Bring to boil, cover and simmer 1 hour. Remove cover and simmer 1 hour longer.

Remove veal from pan. Raise heat and reduce sauce to about 4 cups. Mix water with cornstarch and add to sauce, cooking until sauce thickens slightly. Return veal to pan and heat through. Serve with polenta.

Polenta

4 cups chicken stock
2 cups polenta
1 cup heavy cream
2 Tbsps. butter

2 tsps. salt
2 tsps. pepper
1 cup Parmesan cheese,
   grated

In a large saucepan bring chicken stock to boil. Lower heat and slowly stir in polenta, cooking for 4 to 5 minutes. Stir constantly. Stir in cream, butter, salt and pepper. Cook 1 minute, stirring constantly. Blend in Parmesan cheese and serve immediately.

Tiramisú

Preparation Time: 1½ Hours

   8 oz. mascarpone cheese
   3 eggs
   3 Tbsps. sugar
2¼ cups espresso coffee
  ⅓ cup rum
   8 oz. lady fingers
   3 Tbsps. unsweetened cocoa powder

In a medium bowl gently mix cheese, eggs and sugar until smooth and thoroughly blended. Refrigerate.

In another bowl, combine coffee and rum. Quickly dip half the lady fingers, one at a time, into coffee mixture.

Arrange in an even layer on the bottom of a glass dish or non-aluminum pan about 8 × 10 × 2". Cover with half the cheese mixture. Repeat layers. Smooth top and sift cocoa over the top to a depth of about ⅛" thick. Cover with plastic or foil and refrigerate at least 1 hour.

Cut into squares to serve.

BENKAY RESTAURANT

JAPANESE
222 Mason Street
394-1105
Monday—Friday Breakfast 7AM—9AM
Lunch Noon—2PM
Dinner 6PM—9:30PM
Saturday-Sunday dinner only 6PM—9:30PM
AVERAGE DINNER FOR TWO: $90

As YOU STEP into the Benkay, the sweeping San Francisco skyline greets you. Benkay, the Japanese restaurant located on the 25th floor of Hotel Nikko, is a unique blending of the traditional and contemporary. From the serenity of the raked sand garden, the sleek modern sushi bar and the beauty of the kimono-clad waitresses, Benkay offers the best of Japan.

The western-style dining room, a relaxing hideaway high above the hustle and bustle of Union Square, features a complete menu with ala carte items as well as set dinners. The sushi bar offers the freshest selections available. For the more adventurous, traditional tatami rooms are available featuring Kaiseki menu. Kaiseki, based on the tea ceremony, is the ancient art of blending courses to harmonize flavor, color and texture.

Benkay offers a unique dining experience—a contemporary example of East meeting West.

Authentic Japanese Cuisine

Chef Naoyuki Miyagawa's Menu for Four

Rolled Smoked Salmon Asparagus
Japanese Style Fried Chicken
Roast Duck Filet with Mustard Sauce
Lobster Teriyaki
Crab Meat with Hollandaise Sauce

Rolled Smoked Salmon Asparagus

Preparation Time: 15 Minutes

8 stems of asparagus
4 slices smoked salmon

Steam the asparagus, but do not overcook. After the asparagus has cooled down, wrap or roll 2 stems of asparagus into a slice of smoked salmon.

Slice the asparagus-wrapped salmon diagonally and chill in the refrigerator until ready to serve.

Japanese Style Fried Chicken

Preparation Time: 20 Minutes

1 lb. chicken breast filet
1 cup soy sauce
¾ cup corn starch
Vegetable oil

Slice the chicken filet into bite-size pieces and marinate in the soy sauce for approximately 5 minutes.

Drain the chicken pieces and coat with corn starch. Shake off any extra corn starch from the chicken and deep fry in 340° vegetable oil.

Serve 5 pieces per person while the chicken is hot.

Roast Duck Filet with Mustard Sauce

Preparation Time: 1 ½ Hours

1½ lbs. duck filet
Dash of salt
½ cup soy sauce
¼ cup fish broth
2 Tbsps. Japanese mustard
Garnish of asparagus or broccoli

Sprinkle salt on the duck filet and refrigerate for 1 hour.

Make a cold sauce by combining the soy sauce, fish broth and Japanese mustard.

Skewer the duck filet and grill over heat, turning a few times to cook medium-well. Take out the skewers and slice the duck.

Place the duck slices on a small plate and pour the sauce over the duck.

Garnish with steamed asparagus or broccoli.

Lobster Teriyaki

Preparation Time: 30 Minutes

2½ **cups sake**
3½ **cups Mirin (Japanese cooking wine)**
2½ **cups soy sauce**
 ½ **cup sugar**
 2 **fresh lobsters**

Simmer the sake, Mirin, soy sauce and sugar over low heat until the teriyaki sauce is reduced 25%. Cool the sauce to room temperature.

Cut the lobsters into 4 halves and grill over high heat until the lobster is half-way cooked. Dip the lobster into the teriyaki sauce a few times and grill again on low heat.

Serve hot.

Cooking tip: Refrigerate the teriyaki sauce in a tightly sealed container or bottle. The sauce can be kept for long periods of time if you keep re-heating it every two weeks.

Crab Meat with Hollandaise Sauce

Preparation Time: 20 Minutes

5 egg yolks
2 Tbsps. rice vinegar
1 Tbsp. vegetable oil
1 Tbsp. sugar
Pinch of salt
¾ cup crab meat, cooked

Combine the egg yolks, rice vinegar, oil, sugar and salt in a double-boiler and stir until the sauce becomes creamy. Remove from heat and cool to room temperature.

Place crab meat in a small bowl and pour the hollandaise sauce over it.

Yamato Restaurant & Sushi Bar

JAPANESE
717 California Street
397-3456
Lunch Tuesday–Friday 11:45AM–2PM
Dinner Tuesday–Sunday 5PM–10PM
AVERAGE DINNER FOR TWO: $35

THE RESTAURANT'S INTERIOR was handcrafted in Japan, using 40 varieties of wood and 13 varieties of bamboo, then broken down and reassembled on its present California Street location. Inside Yamato, "the mountain gate," beautiful ikebana fresh flower sculptures, decorative scrolls, Japanese artifacts and original wood carvings enhance the setting. Miniature gardens and the classic Uguisi Bari bridge (it makes a warning squeak when crossed) add to the decor.

Kimono-clad waitresses serve your meal either at Western tables or in the Japanese tatami rooms.

Yamato is a consistent winner of Travel/Holiday magazine and Mobil four star awards. Its success and loyal following among Westerners as well as the many Japanese who dine here speaks for itself.

SINCE 1946 yamato

Chef Joe Ishizaki's Menu for Four

Miso Shiru (Soybean Soup)
Nasu Hasami Yaki (Eggplant Chicken Appetizer)
Sunomono (Vegetable Salad)
Tempura (Seafood & Vegetables)
Sukiyaki (Beef Vegetable Dish)

Soybean Soup

Preparation Time: 10 Minutes

3 ½ cups dashi (Japanese fish stock)
4 Tbsps. red miso
½ cake tofu in ½" cubes
4 Tbsps. green onions, chopped
  Sansho pepper

Heat the dashi in a saucepan.

Put the miso into a small bowl and gradually add 4 Tbsps. of the dashi, beating continuously with a wire whisk to dissolve the miso. Stir the dissolved miso back into the soup, being sure there are no lumps.

As the soup simmers, add the tofu. Do not boil.

Pour servings of soup into individual bowls and spinkle with green onion and small pinches of sansho pepper.

Eggplant Chicken Appetizer

Preparation Time: 20 Minutes
Pre-heat oven to 400°

   4 Japanese eggplants 5" each (or 1 medium eggplant)
   4 chicken breast filets, 1" wide, boned and skinned
   ⅓ cup soy sauce
   5 tsps. sugar
   1 oz. Mirin (Japanese wine), sake or sherry
   2 tsps. cornstarch
   1 tsp. ginger, fresh or powdered
   Garnish with shredded lettuce and tomato

Remove stems of Japanese eggplants. Make a shallow cut around the eggplant 1½" from the stem end. Leave skin on stem end, peel balance of the skin. Split the eggplant on the peeled end only. If using Italian eggplant, follow same procedure but quarter lengthwise.

To make yakitori sauce, heat soy sauce and sugar. Add Mirin, cornstarch and ginger and bring to a boil.

Fit the two halves of the butterflied eggplants around the filets. Place on oiled cookie sheet and bake for 12 minutes or until tender.

Baste with yakitori sauce and serve.

Vegetable Salad

Preparation Time: 10 Minutes (note marinading time)

1½ **lbs. cucumbers, peeled, thinly sliced**
¾ **tsp. salt**
¾ **cup cider vinegar**
½ **cup sugar**
¾ **tsp. MSG, optional**
   Garnish of cooked crab, shrimp, tomato slices

Sprinkle cucumbers with salt. Allow to stand at room temperature for one hour.

Thoroughly blend together remaining ingredients for dressing, stirring until sugar dissolves.

Add ⅓ cup of the dressing to the cucumbers. Stir lightly and drain.

Before serving, pour remaining dressing over cucumbers. Serve in individual bowls and garnish with cooked crab, small shrimp and tomato slices.

Tempura

Preparation Time: 35 Minutes (note refrigeration time)

¾ lb. fish filets, sea bass, petrale, halibut
12 shrimp or prawns
 6 scallops
 1 sweet potato or 3 carrots
 1 small eggplant or 2 zucchini
¼ lb. green beans or asparagus tips
    Cooking oil for frying
 3 cups cake flour
 1 Tbsp. baking powder
 2 egg yolks, beaten
 2 cups ice water
½ cup dashi (Japanese fish stock)
¼ cup soy sauce
 2 tsps. sugar

Cut fish filets into 1½" × 2" pieces. Clean and butterfly shrimp, leaving the tails on. Drain seafood and vegetables thoroughly, cover and chill.

Sift flour and baking powder together. Add egg yolks and water, beating until smooth.

Pour several inches of oil into an electric wok, deep skillet or fondue pot. Heat to 400°. Dip seafood and vegetables in batter and drain lightly. Fry until lightly browned, 3 minutes. Drain.

In a saucepan combine dashi, soy sauce and sugar to make tempura sauce.

Serve with tempura sauce for dipping and (optional) grated fresh radish.

Cooking tip: Preserve color of fresh vegetables and prevent darkening by sprinkling with lemon juice.

Sukiyaki

Preparation Time: 30 Minutes

1 Tbsp. salad oil
1½ lbs. boneless top sirloin or rib steak, sliced thin
4 medium onions, sliced into chunks
1 cake tofu, cubed
1 small can bamboo shoots, sliced
½ lb. bean sprouts
¾ lb. mushrooms, sliced
4 stalks celery, diagonally cut ½" slices
1 can shirataki noodles

Heat an electric skillet or large heavy frying pan to 300°. Add oil to coat pan. Add half of the vegetables and noodles and half the sauce. Quickly cook the vegetables so they are crisp.

Refill skillet and follow same procedure. Serve immediately with rice.

Sukiyaki Sauce

½ cup soy sauce
¼ cup consomme or beef broth
¼ cup water
1 tsp. sugar
2 tsps. sake

Combine ingredients in a saucepan, stirring until sugar dissolves.

SPLENDIDO'S

MEDITERRANEAN
Embarcadero Center Four
Podium (Third) Level
986-3222
Lunch and dinner served daily 11:30AM–10PM
Bar open until midnight
AVERAGE DINNER FOR TWO: $75

THE INVITING INTERIOR of Splendido's is a mix of architectures reflecting the Mediterranean coast. Moorish arches, Greek grain threshers, rustic French/Italian stone walls, grape arbor ceilings and the pewter-topped bar from Portugal hint at the traditional ambiance to be found within. Touches of Mediterranean blue, sunset pink and muted shades of peach and pomegranate contrast with the hand-painted wormwood cabinetry and hand-hewn beams.

Circular booths and round tables create a social mood. An appetizer menu is served in the canopied outdoor patio and in the bar.

While dining, guests can watch Executive Chef Christopher Majer and his chefs at work in the exhibition kitchen. The menu offers Mediterranean flavors with a contemporary style. The emphasis is on French and Italian cuisine, showing a concern for taste and calories. The healthful, yet satisfying dishes are distinctive in both textures and presentation. All baked goods, breads and desserts are made fresh daily on premises.

Chef Christopher Majer's Menu for Eight

Bresaola with Celery Root Remoulade
Warm Goat Cheese and Ratatouille Salad
Tagliarini with Pesto, Clams & White Beans
Peppered Tuna with Chive Potatoes, Red Wine & Orange
Beaujolais Granite
Black Pepper Butter Cookies

Bresaola

Preparation Time: 10 Minutes

24 pieces bresaola, thinly sliced
6 oz. Caprini cheese
2 oz. Mascarpone cheese
1 egg yolk
1 Tbsp. extra virgin olive oil
   Salt and freshly ground pepper to taste
   Lettuce or herb garnish

Combine both cheeses and egg yolk until smooth. Season with salt and pepper.

Spoon the mixture on the top ⅓ of each sliced meat. Roll the meat around the cheese mixture.

To serve, divide the bresaola among eight plates and arrange in a spoke-like pattern. Place the celery root remoulade in the center of the plate.

Garnish the plate with individual leaves of baby red oak or green leaf lettuce or herbs, placed in the center of the remoulade. Drizzle the bresaola with olive oil and sprinkle with freshly ground black pepper.

Celery Root Remoulade

Preparation Time: 15 Minutes

2 cups celery root, peeled, julienned
¼ cup fresh lemon juice
3 Tbsps. mayonnaise
1 Tbsp. whole-grain mustard
2 tsps. Dijon mustard
1 tsp. shallots, finely chopped
Salt and freshly ground pepper to taste

Toss the celery root with the lemon juice and let stand for 15 minutes.

In a large bowl combine the mayonnaise, mustards and shallots, stirring until well blended.

Add the celery root and season with salt and pepper.

Warm Goat Cheese & Ratatouille Salad

Preparation Time: 45 Minutes
Pre-heat oven to 350°

1 eggplant, medium
1 yellow squash, medium
1 zucchini, medium
1 yellow pepper, small
1 red pepper, small
1 onion, small
1 ripe tomato
2 cloves garlic, minced
2 Tbsps. Italian parsley, chopped
1 tsp. thyme, dried
Olive oil for sautéing
Kosher salt and black pepper to taste
16 oz. goat cheese
4 tsps. Nicoise olives, chopped
2 bunch arugula
1 head frisee (chicory lettuce)
1 small head radicchio
1 shallot, peeled and minced
1 Tbsp. Dijon mustard
3 Tbsps. red wine vinegar
5 oz. virgin olive oil

To make the ratatouille, dice and sauté all the vegetables in olive oil separately, finishing each with a little of the garlic, thyme, salt and pepper.

Transfer to a baking dish and bake uncovered at 350° for 15–20 minutes. Add half of the parsley and check for seasoning.

While the ratatouille is baking, combine the arugula, frisee, radicchio, shallots and the other half of the parsley. Make a vinaigrette by combining mustard, vinegar, salt and pepper. Whisk in olive oil and season to taste. Dress the greens with the vinaigrette and set aside.

In 4 oz. ramekins or aluminum cups press in 2 oz. goat cheese. Top with ratatouille. Heat in 450° oven until warm, approximately 1 to 2 minutes.

To serve, unmold the ramekins on a large plate, placing the dressed greens around them. Place a little of the chopped olives centered on top of the goat cheese.

Tagliarini with Pesto, Clams & White Beans

Preparation Time: 35 Minutes

¾ cups basil leaves, tightly packed
¼ cup Italian parsley leaves
2 Tbsps. pine nuts
3 cloves garlic, peeled
2 Tbsps. Pecorino romano cheese, grated
2 Tbsps. Reggiano Parmesan cheese, grated
⅔ cup virgin olive oil
18 oz. fresh tagliarini
2 lbs. manila or small littleneck clams, rinsed
¼ cup white wine
½ cup chicken broth
1 pint white beans, cooked
Kosher salt and freshly ground pepper to taste

Place the first 4 ingredients in a food processor and blend to a medium consistency to make the pesto. Fold in grated cheeses. Season with salt and pepper.

Bring a pot of salted water to a boil and add the pasta, cooking until al dente, or firm. Drain.

While pasta is cooking, poach the clams in the white wine and chicken stock, adding more stock if necessary. When the clams open, add the pesto and white beans.

Combine the pasta and sauce, garnishing with grated cheese if desired.

Peppered Tuna with Chive Potatoes, Red Wine & Orange

Preparation Time: 45 Minutes

 8 tuna steaks, ¾" thick
 1 bottle red wine
 1 qt. veal stock
 5 shallots, peeled, chopped
 5 garlic cloves, chopped
15 black peppercorns
 1 sprig tarragon
 3 Tbsps. butter, unsalted
 1 egg white
 2 Tbsps. cracked black pepper
 6 medium russet potatoes
 ½ cup heavy cream
 ½ cup crème fraiche
 2 chives, finely chopped
   Salt and pepper to taste
   Olive oil
   Zest of orange

In a large pot combine the wine, veal stock, shallots, garlic, pepper-corns and tarragon. Cook over medium heat until reduced by three quarters. Whisk in butter, strain and season to taste.

Brush the tuna steaks with egg white and gently press in cracked black pepper. Set aside.

Peel and cut potatoes into sixths and place in cold water. Cook until soft. Drain and run through a food mill or press through a sieve. Mix in heavy cream, creme fraiche and chives. Season with salt and pepper. Set aside.

In a large frying pan season the tuna with salt and sear in olive oil until cooked, rare.

To serve, place the potatoes in the center of the plate and top with tuna. Distribute the orange zest around the potatoes and tuna. Pour the red wine sauce over the orange zest.

Beaujolais Granite

Preparation Time: 1½ Hours

   1 bottle Beaujolais
   1 lime
   1 orange
   1 lemon
   1 cup sugar
   2 Tbsps. water
     Strawberries for garnish

In a large cooking pan, combine the zest and juice from the lime, orange and lemon with the sugar and water. Heat to dissolve. Add the wine and heat until warm.

Pour the wine mixture into a shallow pan and place in the freezer. Every 20 minutes use a balloon whip to break up the ice into chips. The whole process will take about 1½ hours.

Serve in a wine glass or large martini glass with quartered strawberries and black pepper butter cookies.

Black Pepper Butter Cookies

Preparation Time: 15 Minutes (note refrigeration time)
Yield: 2 dozen

  8 oz. of butter, cut and cubed
½ cup sugar
  2 cups flour
  2 eggs
    Dash of vanilla
    Freshly ground black pepper
  2 Tbsps. sugar

In a large bowl, cream the butter, sugar and flour until fluffy. Add one egg and vanilla and blend well. Fold in the flour and mix to a dough-like consistency. Refrigerate the dough for two hours.

Remove the dough from the refrigerator and roll out to approximately ¼" thick. Sprinkle liberally with black pepper, pressing it gently into the dough with the rolling pin. Cut out dough with cookie cutter and place on baking paper. Refrigerate for 30 minutes.

Make an egg wash by beating one egg with a little water. Brush the egg wash over the cookies and sprinkle lightly with sugar.

Bake at 325° for 5–7 minutes.

CORONA BAR & GRILL

MEXICAN
88 Cyril Magnin Street
392-5500
Lunch and dinner Monday–Saturday 11:30AM–11PM
Lunch and dinner Sunday Noon–11PM
Bar open until midnight
AVERAGE DINNER FOR TWO: $40–$50

THIS IS HIGH-ENERGY, fun-loving, true Mexican cuisine at its best. The menu interprets regional Mexican cooking with an emphasis on the coastal area's seafood dishes. The chef's trademarks are bright, clean intense flavors and fresh, frequently organic ingredients.

Seafood appetizers offer tempting delicacies such as ceviche verde of crab, shrimp in chipotle and Yucatan-style pepper oysters. The daily selection of fresh fish grilled over hardwood, such as yellowfin tuna with tomatillo chipotle salsa or swordfish with black chanterelles, are only a few of the tempting entree highlights which may be enjoyed in the dining room or at the 90-foot long, cherrywood bar.

The setting is warm and comfortable with glowing round wall lights that suggest the sun setting over the Pacific Ocean from a Mexican beach. The theme colors are raspberry, teal and rosy sunset pink. A wonderful collection of handcrafted Mexican masks hangs above the bar, with larger pieces decorating the wall throughout the restaurant.

Corona Bar & Grill

Chef Tom Fox's Menu for Four

Ceviche of Ahi Tuna with Papaya and Avocado
Salad of Shaved Radishes, Apples, Oranges, Dry Jack Cheese
Herbed Texas Venison in Ancho Pomegranate Sauce
Tamale of Sweet Corn
Pumpkin Guava Pie

Ceviche of Ahi Tuna with Papaya and Avocado

Preparation Time: 35 Minutes

¼ cup lime juice
1 tsp. orange zest
1 tsp. sugar
2 Tbsps. tamarind paste dissolved in 2 Tbsps. warm water
1 shallot
1 clove garlic, chopped
½ tsp. kosher salt
1 Tbsp. chipotle en adobo, pureéd
12 oz. sushi-quality tuna
¼ cup English cucumber, julienned
¼ cup red bell pepper, julienned
1 tsp. sesame seeds, toasted
2 mint leaves
16 cilantro leaves
8 avocado wedges
8 papaya wedges

Combine first eight ingredients to make marinade. Set aside.

Cut tuna into 1 × ¼" slices and toss with 4 tablespoons marinade. Add cucumbers, bell peppers and sesame seeds.

Arrange the avocado and papaya wedges in fans on individual plates, top with tuna and vegetables. Garnish with herbs. Serve immediately.

Salad of Shaved Radishes, Apples, Oranges, Dry Jack Cheese

Preparation Time: 10 Minutes

10 radishes
1 pippin apple
2 tangerines, sectioned, seeded, peeled
1 Tbsp. walnut oil
2 oz. dry jack cheese

Shave the radishes and apples with a Japanese vegetable cutter or a cheese or truffle shaver, into thin long pieces.

Toss the radishes and apples with the tangerines and any remaining juices. Add the walnut oil and toss.

Arrange fruit in the center of individual plates. Shave cheese on top and serve.

Herbed Texas Venison

Preparation Time: 45 Minutes (note refrigeration time)

  1 sprig rosemary
 10 sage leaves
  6 juniper berries
  4 Tbsps. pepper (Tellicherry)
  6 allspice berries
  2 Tbsps. kosher salt
  2 leeks, sliced in rings
  8 green garlic, cut in rings with tops
  1 leg Texas venison, trimmed and butterflied
 ½ cup pomegranate syrup or prickly pear pureé
 ¼ cup light olive oil

Pound herbs together with spices, leek and garlic in a mortar until smooth. Add prickly pear syrup to the marinade.

Rub the venison leg with the marinade and then olive oil. Marinate at room temperature for 4 hours and then overnight under refrigeration. Grill.

Ancho Pomegranate Sauce

 ½ gallon venison stock
 ¼ cup wild mushrooms, diced
    Game herb garni
  5 seeded ancho chiles, soaked, pureéd
  1 cup pomegranate juice

Combine the stock, wild mushrooms, herb garni and chiles in a non-reactive pan and reduce very slowly, skimming often. Cook until reduced by ⅓. Add pomegranate juice and continue to reduce slowly, until a light glaze is formed. Add chiles to the sauce and pass through a sieve.

Tamale of Sweet Corn, Dry Jack Cheese and White Truffles

Preparation Time: 30 Minutes

1½ cups milk
1½ cups water
 ¾ cup corn meal
 2 cups corn cut from dry roasted ears
 ½ cup butter
 ¼ cup dry jack cheese, grated
10 corn husks
 1 white truffle

Boil milk and water together. Stir in the corn meal and cook until smooth, creamy and thick. Stir in corn kernels and butter. Stir in cheese. Let cool.

Wrap mixture in corn husks to form tamales, tying both ends with strips of corn husks.

Steam tamales for 10 minutes to warm through. Open tamales and garnish with shaved white truffles.

Serve with venison.

Pumpkin Guava Pie

Preparation Time: One hour (note refrigeration time)
Pre-heat oven to 350°

1 cup pumpkin, peeled, diced	2 tsps. cinnamon
4 large eggs	1 cup whipping cream
1 cup brown sugar	¼ cup rum

Blanch pumpkin in boiling water until tender. Set aside.

Mix pumpkin, eggs, sugar and cinnamon together. Beat in cream and rum. Spread the praline over the bottom of a prebaked pie shell. (see recipe below) Fold the pumpkin mixture into the baked pie shell. Bake at 350° until brown and set, about 40 minutes.

Praline

3 cups sugar	½ cup milk
1½ cups brown sugar	2 tsps. vanilla extract
3 Tbsps. corn syrup	2 cups pecan halves
4½ oz. butter	

Boil the first six ingredients together, stirring until dissolved. Continue boiling until 250° on a candy thermometer. Pour into a bowl over pecans. Let cool slightly and stir. Set aside for pie.

Guava Ice Cream

3½ cups sugar	9 cups whipping cream
4½ cups half and half	4 cups guavas, pureéd
24 egg yolks	

Scald cream. Whisk sugar and egg yolks together and stir into half and half and cream. Cool until thick. Whisk in guava pureé. Freeze.

AQUA

SEAFOOD
252 California Street
Between Battery & Front Streets
956-9662
Dinner Monday–Thursday 5:30–10:30PM
Friday & Saturday until 11PM
AVERAGE DINNER FOR TWO: $80

The dramatic interior of Aqua reflects the culinary genius of Chef George Morrone and his innovative seafood dishes. The restaurant is on a grand scale with high ceilings, a towering white maple and glass entry door with an appropriate bronze fish tail handle and a 32-foot-long maple bar that carries out the sculpted, curved motif of the room. Even the flower arrangements are enormous, flaunting breathtaking arrangements in large stone urns. Salmon and bone colored walls, gentle lighting and a large California landscape by Wade Hoefer warm these spacious surroundings.

Spectacular dishes created by Chef Morrone are a delight for the palate as much as the restaurant's decor is for the eyes. Unique combinations of seafood, sauces, vegetables and fruits transcend the ranks of the ordinary.

First courses include a Savory Black Mussel Soufflé with Chardonnay, garlic and parsley and Alaskan Prawn Ravioli. Entrées like Medallions of Ahi Tuna pair seafood with foie gras in one of the many daring and delicious combinations that Chef Morrone creates. A Vegetarian Tasting Menu is also available and is a complete five course menu with Clear Carrot Soup, Asparagus Vinaigrette, Wild Mushroom Risotto or Basil Gnocchi, Spinach Soufflé and a Three Melon Terrine. All meals can be enhanced by one of the many wines on the restaurant's wine list. Delicious endings include desserts like the old-fashioned Root Beer Float or the fruity Warm Mango Tart with Pineapple Sorbet and Vanilla Bean Ice Cream.

A Q U A

> ### Chef George Morrone's Menu for Four
>
> *Carpaccio of Wild Salmon*
> *Aqua Crab Cakes*
> *Savory Black Mussel Soufflé*
> *Warm Trout Salad*
> *Chocolate Torte*

Carpaccio of Wild Salmon with Citrus Coriander Seed Vinaigrette

Preparation Time: 30 Minutes (note refrigeration time)

1 whole fresh salmon
½ cup salt
¼ cup sugar
¼ cup coriander seeds, crushed
¼ cup white peppercorns, crushed
3 Tbsps. green peppercorns
1 orange and 1 lemon

2 bunches mint, roughly chopped
3 Tbsps. toasted coriander seeds, pulverized
½ cup extra virgin olive oil
2 Tbsps. shallots, chopped
1 tsp. soy sauce
Lime juice to taste
Salt & pepper to taste

Scale, filet and bone the salmon, leaving the skin on.

In a small mixing bowl, combine the salt, sugar, coriander, white and green peppercorns. Spread this mixture onto the salmon. Squeeze the juice from the orange and lemon, saving the rinds, to yield one cup total. Set aside.

Cut the orange and lemon rinds (with pith) into five strips and place on top of the salmon. Top with mint and tightly wrap the salmon in plastic wrap. Weigh down the salmon between two pans with a couple of large cans. Refrigerate for 24 hours.

To prepare the vinaigrette, sweat the shallots in a small amount of oil, add the reserved citrus juice and reduce over medium heat to ¼ cup. Remove from heat and add the pulverized coriander seeds and soy sauce. Slowly whisk in the olive oil. Add the lime juice, salt and pepper to taste. Set aside.

Remove the salmon from refrigerator and gently brush off the marinade. Thinly slice the filet at an angle and drizzle with the citrus coriander seed vinaigrette.

Aqua Crab Cakes

Preparation Time: 30 Minutes

1 lb. crab meat
1 stalk celery, diced small
½ medium yellow onion, diced small
2 Tbsps. olive oil
2 Tbsps. parsley, chopped
1 Tbsp. chopped chives
1 cup bread crumbs (Panko)
¾ cup mayonnaise (recipe follows)
4 whole eggs, beaten
4 Tbsps. flour
Fresh basil leaves
Fresh tomato, sliced

Lightly sauté the onions and celery in olive oil.

In a mixing bowl, combine the crab, mayonnaise, parsley, chives and ¼ cup bread crumbs. Add the sautéed onion and celery. Form mixture into individual cakes. Lightly dust cakes with flour, shaking off any excess. Dip cakes in the beaten eggs then gently roll cakes in ¾ cup bread crumbs. Shake off any excess breading and chill the prepared cakes until ready to fry.

Coat pan with peanut oil and heat to 360.° Fry the crab cakes until golden brown.

Garnish with fresh basil leaves and sliced tomatoes.

Mayonnaise

Preparation Time: 10 Minutes

 1 **egg yolk**
¾ **cup olive oil**
 1 **tsp. Dijon mustard**
 2 **Tbsps. lemon juice**
⅛ **tsp. cayenne pepper**
   Salt & pepper to taste

In a food processor, blend the egg yolk, mustard, cayenne and lemon juice.

Slowly add the oil in a small, steady stream. Refrigerate.

Savory Black Mussel Soufflé

Preparation Time: 45 Minutes
Preheat oven to 375°

  1 **cup milk**
  6 **Tbsps. butter, sliced**
  6 **Tbsps. all-purpose flour**
  5 **egg yolks**
 16 **mussels**
 ½ **bunch parsley, chopped fine**
  2 **sprigs thyme**
  2 **cups white wine**
  6 **garlic cloves, chopped**
  6 **shallots, chopped**
  7 **egg whites**
    Salt & pepper to taste
  2 **cups heavy cream**

In a saucepan, bring the milk and butter to a boil. Add the flour, reduce heat to low and stir to cook out the flour taste, about 3 to 5 minutes. Transfer the mixture to a bowl and add the yolks one at a time. Mix until cool. Set aside.

Over medium-heat in a heavy saucepan, combine the mussels, 2 Tbsps. parsley, thyme, 1½ cups white wine, and half of the chopped garlic and shallots. Cover the saucepan and steam until mussels open. Pick mussels from shells and reserve the liquid for later use. Chop the mussels into small pieces. Add ½ cup white wine and the remaining shallots and garlic. Reduce until dry. Add the mussels, the egg flour mixture and remaining parsley. Reduce together. Season with salt and pepper. Set aside.

Whip egg whites to soft peak. Fold egg white mixture into the oyster mixture until just combined. Bake in a buttered, floured soufflé mold for 12–15 minutes.

While baking, reduce the reserved mussel liquid to ¼ cup. Add 2 cups of cream and reduce by half. Strain and season with salt and pepper to taste.

Serve the soufflé with the mussel cream sauce.

Warm Trout Salad

Preparation Time: 30 Minutes
Preheat oven to 375°

12 red potatoes, quartered
¼ cup olive oil
 2 Tbsps. rosemary, chopped
    Salt & black pepper to taste
 4 trout, 8 oz. each, deboned, head and tail left on
 4 Tbsps. garlic, purée
 4 tsps. Balsamic vinegar
⅓ cup clarified butter
 4 cups frisée lettuce, cleaned
12 morel mushrooms
16 pearl onions, roasted
16 tiny fingerling potatoes, peeled, roasted
12 green beans, blanched
12 yellow wax beans, blanched
¼ cup tomato concassé
    Warm vinaigrette (recipe follows)
    Bacon reserved from vinaigrette preparation

Toss the potatoes in ¼ cup olive oil, salt, pepper and rosemary. Roast in a 375° oven until tender and golden brown, about 30 minutes.

Sauté trout in clarified butter, garlic purée and Balsamic vinegar until golden.

Gently toss the frisée, bacon, potatoes and vegetables in warm vinaigrette (recipe follows). Top with trout and serve immediately.

Warm Vinaigrette

Preparation Time: 10 Minutes

  3 **shallots, sliced**
¼ **lb. Applewood bacon slices**
  1 **Tbsp. chopped garlic**
  4 **Tbsps. Balsamic vinegar**
  3 **tsps. brown sugar**
½ **cup chicken stock**
¼ **cup olive oil**

    Sauté bacon in olive oil over low heat until cooked. When bacon is cooked, remove from pan and set aside.

    To the sauté pan, add the shallots and cook until soft and slightly browned. Add the garlic, Balsamic vinegar, brown sugar and chicken stock. Reduce by one-third. Check seasonings and adjust to taste.

    Serve dressing warm.

Chocolate Torte

Preparation Time: 45 Minutes
(note refrigeration time)
Preheat oven to 375°

6 oz. dark chocolate, melted
10 Tbsps. butter
½ cup sugar
4 eggs
½ cup all-purpose flour
1¾ Tbsps. cocoa powder
1¾ tsps. baking powder

In a large mixing bowl, blend the butter and sugar. Add the melted chocolate, mixing well. Beat in the eggs one at a time.

In a separate mixing bowl, combine the flour, cocoa powder, and baking powder. Slowly add to the chocolate mixture.

Pour into a ring mold about half full.

Bake for 10 minutes. Remove from oven and chill for 1 hour before serving. Run knife around edge before removing from the mold.

Bentley's Seafood Grill

SEAFOOD
185 Sutter Street
989-6895
Lunch and dinner served daily from 11:30AM–10PM
Bar open until 11PM
AVERAGE DINNER FOR TWO: $40–$50

WHERE TO GO for fresh fish? Bentley's of course, which is famous for its excellent variety of oysters on the half-shell and wide assortment of seafood flown in fresh daily. Entree highlights include grilled fish such as yellowfin tuna, salmon and mahi mahi in a variety of sauces. The salads are innovative and the desserts are made fresh on premises daily.

Bentley's is a combination of classic old San Francisco and the Great Gatsby era, suggesting a mood evocative of the '20s, complete with live jazz pianist in the evenings. The restaurant offers a classic oyster bar atmosphere downstairs with its zinc-surfaced bar and brasserie tables. Upstairs is a more elegant dining area overlooking the oyster bar.

SEAFOOD GRILL
& OYSTER BAR

Chef Amey Shaw's Menu for Eight

Crab Cakes with Cole Slaw & Remoulade
Seafood Andouille Sausage Gumbo
Grilled Cured Salmon with Spinach & Honey Mustard Sauce
Grilled Prawns with Cilantro Pesto & Red Pepper Jam
Apple & Blueberry Tartlets with Creme Anglaise

Crab Cakes

Preparation Time: 35 Minutes

   1 lb. crab meat
   1 lb. shrimp, chopped
   ½ cup fine bread crumbs
   1 tsp. cayenne
   ½ tsp. Tabasco
   ¼ cup scallions, chopped
   1 tsp. Worcestershire
   6 eggs
   ½ cup mayonnaise
   ¼ cup water
   2 cups all-purpose flour
   2 cups bread crumbs.
   Oil

Combine the first seven ingredients in a stainless steel bowl. Add one egg and mayonnaise to mixture. Shape mixture into 20 patties ½" thick.

Whip 5 eggs with water. Lightly dust patties with flour, then dip into the egg mixture, then the breadcrumbs. Repeat until all are breaded.

Heat a sauté pan with oil. Place crabcakes in pan, do not crowd, and lightly brown on both sides for about 5 to 6 minutes.

Serve with coleslaw and remoulade on the side.

Cole Slaw

Preparation Time: 10 Minutes

½ head red cabbage, shredded
1 head green cabbage, shredded
1 medium carrot, grated
¼ cup mayonnaise
   Salt and pepper to taste

Mix all ingredients. Add mayonnaise a little at a time. Serve with crab cakes and remoulade.

Remoulade

Preparation Time: 5 Minutes

2 cups mayonnaise
¼ cup cornichons, chopped
¼ cup capers, chopped
1 oz. chives, chopped
1 tsp. paprika
½ tsp. cayenne
1 oz. anchovies, chopped (optional)
   Salt and pepper to taste

Mix together and chill.

Seafood and Andouille Sausage Gumbo

Preparation Time: 1½ Hours

½ lb. Andouille sausage,
    cut into ½" cubes
1 medium onion, diced
1 cup celery, diced
1 cup okra, diced
2 tsp. gumbo file (Bruce's)
1 cup whole canned tomato
2 Tbsps. Worcestershire
1 Tbsp. Tabasco

1 tsp. cayenne
64 oz. clam broth or light
    fish stock
8 jumbo prawns (peeled &
    deveined)
½ lb. snapper, cut into
    ½" cubes
Salt and pepper to taste

In a heavy stainless steel pot, add sausage and cook for 5 minutes, stirring constantly. Add onions and celery, cook 3 minutes. Add okra and gumbo file, cook 5 minutes. Add tomato, Worcestershire, Tabasco, cayenne, and clam broth. Bring to a simmer for 40 minutes. Add roux (see recipe below) a little at time until slightly thickened. Simmer for 15 minutes. Add prawns and snapper. Cook for 5 minutes. Check seasonings. Serve in bowls with rice.

Red Roux

1 cup peanut oil
¾ cup all-purpose flour

Heat oil in a heavy stainless steel pot until smoking. Add flour slowly, stirring constantly. Stir until roux is reddish brown. Remove from heat and transfer to another pot to cool.

Cooking tip: Roux should be made at least 1 hour before the soup to allow it to cool. Moisture in the flour will cause steam and splattering when added to the hot oil.

Grilled Cured Salmon with Spinach & Honey Mustard Sauce

Preparation Time: 15 Minutes (note refrigeration time)

1 cup kosher salt
2 cups sugar
2 bunches tarragon,
   chopped
Black pepper
¼ cup tequila
2 lbs. salmon

4 bunches spinach,
   cleaned
1 medium carrot,
   cut in 1" long slivers
1 small red onion,
   thinly sliced

Combine the salt, sugar, tarragon and pepper to make marinade. Place the salmon in a shallow pan and spread half the marinade on top, covering it completely. Marinate 24 hours.

Wipe off old marinade and pour tequila evenly over salmon. Spread remaining marinade on top. Cover with plastic wrap. Marinate 24 hours.

Wipe off all the marinade and slice on a bias. Lightly grill each piece, just to heat through.

Evenly distribute spinach onto salad plates, placing the salmon on top. Drizzle entire salad with the honey mustard sauce. Garnish with carrots and red onions.

Honey Mustard Sauce

¼ cup honey
¼ cup grainy mustard
2 Tbsps. Dijon mustard
½ cup clam broth
   Salt and pepper

Combine honey and both mustards in a mixer on high. Slowly add the clam broth until you have a light pourable sauce. Check for seasonings.

228

Grilled Prawns with Cilantro Pesto and Red Pepper Jam

Preparation Time: 45 Minutes (note soaking time)

  1 small onion, diced
  1 tsp. garlic, chopped
  2 Tbsps. olive oil
  2 cups white beans, soaked overnight
  ½ cup white wine
  3 cups clam broth
40 jumbo prawns, peeled and deveined

Sauté onion and garlic in the olive oil. Drain the beans and add to the onion mixture. Add wine and clam broth. Simmer until beans are tender, about 25 minutes.

Skewer the prawns on bamboo skewers, 5 prawns per person. Lightly oil and grill for 6 minutes or until cooked medium. Remove from skewers.

Spoon 3 oz. of beans onto the center of individual plates. Place a spoon of cilantro pesto around the edge of the plate, alternating with the red pepper jam. Arrange prawns in a circle, leaning up against the beans.

Cilantro Pesto

Preparation Time: 10 Minutes

3 bunches cilantro, washed, chopped
1 tsp. fresh ginger, grated
1 Tbsp. sesame seeds
1 cup extra virgin olive oil
   Salt and pepper to taste

Pureé cilantro in a food processor until smooth. Add ginger and sesame seeds and pureé. Slowly add the oil until you have a slightly thick mixture. Season with salt and pepper.

Red Pepper Jam

Preparation Time: 10 Minutes

1 tsp. garlic, chopped
1 Tbsp. olive oil
4 red peppers, roasted, diced
   Salt and pepper to taste

Sauté the garlic in oil. Add the peppers, cooking over medium low heat for 5 minutes. Season with salt and pepper.

Apple & Blueberry Tartlets with Creme Anglaise

Preparation Time: 1½ Hours (note refrigeration time)
Pre-heat oven to 375°

4 cups flour	8 apples, sliced
½ tsp. baking powder	1 cup blueberries
1½ cup sugar	1 tsp. nutmeg
½ lb. butter, chilled	1 tsp. allspice
Grated rind of 2 lemons	1 orange rind, grated
2 eggs	Egg wash (1 egg beaten
3 Tbsps. milk	with 1 Tbsp. water)

Sift together flour, baking powder and ½ cup sugar. Add butter and knead into flour until crumbly. Add lemon rind.

In a separate bowl, beat eggs and milk. Combine with flour mixture and knead. Chill for 2 hours.

Make the filling by combining 1 cup sugar with apples, blueberries, nutmeg, allspice and orange rind over medium heat, until fruit is cooked through.

Roll out dough and line tartlet molds on the bottom and sides. Spoon in filling and top with dough, moistening the edges to seal. Glaze with an egg wash and sprinkle of sugar. Bake at 375° for 45 minutes. Serve tartlets warm with Creme Anglaise on the side.

Creme Anglaise

2 Tbsps. sugar	1 cup milk
Pinch of salt	½ tsp. vanilla
4 large egg yolks	1 Tbsp. Grand Marnier

Stir together sugar, salt and yolks. Heat milk and vanilla to boiling point. Add sugar mixture, stirring constantly. Heat just to below boiling point. Allow to cool. Add Grand Marnièr.

HAYES STREET GRILL

SEAFOOD
320 Hayes Street
863-5545
Monday–Thursday 11:30AM–10PM
Friday 11:30AM–11PM
Saturday 6PM–11PM
AVERAGE DINNER FOR TWO: $50

THE HAYES STREET GRILL has been a local favorite for over ten years. This popular restaurant is noted for fresh fish grilled over mesquite, innovative and seasonal salads and interesting desserts. The wine list offers an affordable collection of excellent California wines.

The decor is simple and comfortable and the service is superb. Hayes Street Grill is the perfect place for a pre-concert dinner, a family celebration, or simply a great meal.

Chef Jacquelyn Buchanan's Menu for Six

Steamed Clams in Chinese Black Bean Sauce
Grilled Calamari & Artichoke Salad
Grilled Salmon with Buerre Blanc
Creme Brulée

Steamed Clams in Chinese Black Bean Sauce

Preparation Time: 30 Minutes

3 Tbsps. peanut oil
2 Tbsps. garlic, minced
2 Tbsps. fresh ginger, grated
2 Tbsps. Chinese fermented black beans
2 Tbsps. dry sherry
½ tsp. dried red chile flakes
3 lbs. clams, soaked in cold water, drained
2 cups chicken stock
4 scallions, sliced thin
¼ cup soy sauce
1 Tbsp. sesame oil

Heat peanut oil in a wok or pot large enough to accommodate the clams when opened. Add the garlic, ginger, black beans, sherry and chile flakes and sauté until fragrant, but do not let the garlic brown. Put the clams in the pot and add the chicken stock. Bring to a simmer and cover. Cook until clams open.

Add half the sliced scallions, soy sauce and sesame oil. Divide clams and broth into 6 bowls. Garnish with remaining scallions.

Grilled Calamari & Artichoke Salad

Preparation Time: 30 Minutes (note marinating time)

 3 cloves garlic, minced
 2 Tbsps. lemon juice
 ¼ cup olive oil
   Salt and pepper
1½ lb. calamari, cleaned
 1 red pepper, julienned
 1 yellow pepper, julienned
 1 Tbsp. capers
 ½ cup celery or fennel, thinly sliced
 1 red onion, thinly sliced
 2 cups arugula lettuce
   Marinated baby artichokes
   Garnish of nicoise olives, lemon wedges

In a large bowl whisk the garlic, lemon juice, olive oil, salt and pepper to make the marinade. Marinate the calamari for at least 30 minutes or up to 3 hours.

Toss remaining ingredients in a large salad bowl. Set aside.

Grill the marinated calamari and slice into rings. Toss with the salad and add enough dressing (see following recipe) to coat. Garnish with olives and lemon wedges.

Italian Dressing

Preparation Time: 5 Minutes

¼ cup lemon juice
¼ cup red wine vinegar
2 tsps. Worcestershire sauce
1 tsp. salt
¼ tsp. pepper
1 cup extra virgin olive oil
¼ cup fresh basil, chopped
2 Tbsps. fresh parsley, chopped
3 cloves garlic, minced

Combine the lemon juice, red wine vinegar and Worcestershire sauce in a stainless bowl. Add the salt and pepper.

Whisk in the olive oil and chopped herbs.

Grilled Salmon with Buerre Blanc

Preparation Time: 30 Minutes

½ cup white wine vinegar
2 Tbsps. dry vermouth
2 Tbsps. lemon juice
2 Tbsps. shallots, finely chopped
1 ½ cups butter, cut into pieces
    Salt and white pepper to taste
Six 8 oz. portions salmon filets
    Olive oil

Put vinegar, vermouth, lemon juice and shallots into a heavy-bottomed saucepan. Bring to a boil and reduce until 2 Tbsps. are left.

Remove the pan from the heat and begin whisking the butter pieces into the reduction, one or two at a time. Turn the heat to very low and return the pan to the heat. Continue to whisk in the butter until all is incorporated. The sauce should be the consistency of heavy cream. Season to taste with salt and pepper.

Oil fish lightly after salting and peppering lightly. Grill over mesquite to desired doneness.

Serve salmon with buerre blanc sauce.

Cooking tip: The addition of 2 Tbsps. of chopped chives or basil is optional.

Creme Brulée

Preparation Time: 2½ Hours (note refrigeration time)
Pre-heat oven to 250°

8 egg yolks
⅓ cup granulated sugar
3 cups whipping cream
Brown sugar

Beat egg yolks and granulated sugar together. Set aside.

Over high heat, scald the whipping cream and add the cream to the egg mixture slowly, stirring constantly.

Divide the mixture between the ramekins. Place the ramekins in a pan and add water to the pan to come half way up the side of the ramekins.

Bake the creme brulée in a 250° oven for 1½ to 2 hours. The mixture should not be runny in the center.

Remove from pan and cool completely. Refrigerate.

Cover the cold custard with a thin layer of brown sugar. Place the ramekins under a pre-heated broiler until the sugar melts and begins to caramelize.

Serve when the sugar has cooled.

Cooking tip: Creme brulée should be eaten within 2 hours of melting sugar.

ALEJANDRO'S

SOUTH AMERICAN
1840 Clement Street
668-1184
Dinner Monday–Thursday 5PM–11PM
Friday–Saturday 5PM–Midnight
Sunday 4PM–11PM
AVERAGE DINNER FOR TWO: $35

ALEJANDRO'S TRANSPORTS YOU to South America, featuring Spanish, Mexican and Peruvian cuisine.

The experience begins when you hear the Spanish guitarist as you enter the white-stucco dining room. The atmosphere is fun and casual.

Elaborate antique mirrors adorn the walls and large Spanish chandeliers hang from the beamed ceiling.

The menu is innovative, offering large, platter-sized dinners at a reasonable price. The tapas, Spanish appetizers, are superb at Alejandro's.

Alejandro's
·SOCIEDAD GASTRONOMICA·

Chef Alejandro Espinosa's Menu for Eight

Jicama Salad
Prawn Soup
Cheese & Jalapeño Eggroll with Dipping Sauce
Paella
Brown Custard

Jicama Salad

Preparation Time: 30 Minutes (note refrigeration time)

12 seedless oranges
2 red onions, chopped
1 large jicama, chopped
1½ cups cilantro, chopped fine
   Salt to taste
   Chile powder to taste

Peel and separate oranges into wedges. Mix the oranges with the remaining ingredients.

Refrigerate for 2 hours before serving.

Prawn Soup

Preparation Time: One hour

3 Tbsps. vegetable oil
1 tomato, peeled, diced
1 onion, diced
1 yellow chile, diced small
3 cloves garlic, diced
   Salt and pepper to taste
   Pinch of marjoram
   Pinch of oregano
3¾ qts. water
16 large prawns
1 lb. yellow potatoes
½ cup peas
½ cup corn
½ cup rice
3 eggs
2 dried chiles, seeded, julienned
1 cup evaporated milk
2 Tbsps. parsley, chopped

Pour oil into a large soup pot over high heat and add the tomato pieces to brown. Add the onion, yellow chiles, garlic, salt, pepper, marjoram and oregano, stirring constantly. Reduce the heat and add the water and prawns.

Dice 2 yellow potatoes into small pieces. Add to the soup mixture along with the peas, corn and rice. Cook over a low flame until the rice is almost done, then add the rest of the potatoes cut in half.

When the soup is cooked, add the eggs without beating them. The eggs will coagulate in large pieces. Add the dried chiles, milk and parsley. Stir and serve.

(Alejandrinos) Cheese & Jalapeño Eggroll with Dipping Sauce

Preparation Time: 25 Minutes

2 eggs
½ lb. Monterey jack cheese,
   grated
1 Tbsp. jalapeño peppers,
   chopped

2 Tbsps. cilantro, chopped
3 scallions, chopped
1 package won ton wraps
   Vegetable oil

Over medium heat, scramble the eggs. When cooked, add the cheese, jalapeño peppers, cilantro and scallions. Mix well and remove from heat and cool.

Place egg mixture in individual won tons and seal edges by pinching firmly.

Deep fry in oil until golden brown on both sides.

Dipping Sauce

2 cups mayonnaise
¼ cup black olives,
   chopped
¼ cup dill relish
3 scallions, chopped
2 Tbsps. parsley, chopped

1 Tbsp. capers
1 Tbsp. caper vinegar
   (caper juice)
½ cup ketchup
   Juice of one lemon
   Salt and pepper to taste

Mix all ingredients well and refrigerate before serving.

Cooking tip: Alejandrinos can be deep fried a few hours ahead and kept warm in a covered pan in the oven.

Paella

Preparation Time: 1 ½ Hours

½ cup olive oil
2 cloves, garlic, pressed
1 onion, diced
1 tomato, chopped
1 bell pepper, julienned
8 pieces chicken, 4 oz. each
2 cups long-grain rice
4 cups water
1 Dungeness crab
8 prawns
8 steamer clams in shells
6 calamari, cut into 1" pieces
6 links chorizo (Spanish sausage)
2 whole bay leaves
½ tsp. salt
¼ tsp. white pepper
Dash Spanish saffron, threads or powder

Heat the olive oil in a heavy skillet and brown the garlic. Add the onion, tomato and bell pepper. Add the chicken to brown.

Stir in the rice, then add the water. Turn the flame to high and bring the paella to a boil.

Add the seafood and chorizo and seasonings. Reduce the heat and simmer for 30 to 45 minutes.

Brown Custard

Preparation Time: One hour

1 cup sugar
2 cups dark brown sugar
½ cup water
1 tsp. bicarbonate of soda
½ gal. milk
2 Tbsps. cornstarch

Prepare a syrup with the sugar, brown sugar and water. Add the milk, cornstarch and bicarbonate of soda, bringing the custard to a boil. Allow to thicken, stirring constantly.

The custard is ready when it becomes dark in color and the bottom of the saucepan can be seen when stirring.

Serve cold.

Old mansion at the corner of Washington Street and Van Ness Avenue

Unforgettable Places to Stay

To a large degree, the pleasure you find in San Francisco depends on your accommodations. That's why "San Francisco's Secrets" turns now to the secret hideaways that make this city so memorable.

We have hand-picked 15 inns that we heartily recommend. The selected inns and hotels were chosen because they are so enchanting, so perfect in ambiance and service that you will luxuriate in their surroundings.

Included are historic mansions with only six guest rooms, romantic bed and breakfast inns and luxurious hotels that offer services designed to pamper their guests.

Each of the inns submits a treasured recipe from among its repertoire.

In addition, you'll learn some of the legends that make this historic city so fascinating.

Recommended Inns

Alamo Square Inn 248	Petite Auberge 262
Archbishops Mansion Inn . 250	Queen Anne Hotel 266
Campton Place Hotel 252	Sherman House 268
Four Seasons Clift Hotel . . . 254	Spencer House 270
Inn at the Opera 256	Victorian Inn on the Park . 274
Inn San Francisco 258	Westin St. Francis 276
The Majestic 260	White Swan Inn 278

ACCORDING TO LEGEND...

It's somewhat confusing—North Beach now has no beach, Telegraph Hill no telegraph and the word is, Coit Tower was not modeled after a firehose nozzle, as is commonly believed.

North Beach got its name from a vanished beach at Francisco Street, before achieving its worldwide fame in the 1950's. The district became a mecca for artists and writers who called themselves the "beats."

Telegraph Hill was so named because it was the location of a semaphore station linked by telegraph to the Western shore. Ships arriving into the harbor would telegraph the station, which would signal the townspeople. Today, it is the site of Coit Tower.

In 1934 the architect of City Hall, Arthur Brown Jr., designed Coit Tower. Rumor has it that Lillie Hitchcock Coit, a celebrity as a teenager for her constant attendance at fires, became the mascot and honorary member of Knickerbocker Engine Co. #5. Lillie left one-third of her estate to the city of San Francisco, for the purpose of adding to the city's beauty. The Coit Advisory Committee commissioned two monuments—a bronze statue in memory of the original volunteer fire department and an observatory tower on Telegraph Hill.

The Powell Street cable car, circa 1890

Old Chinatown: Ornate architecture and men wearing long queues

GOUGH AND OCTAVIA streets were named after a milkman, Charles H. Gough, in the 1850's. Gough, worked his route on a horse with milk cans tied to the saddle. Contrary to popular myth, Octavia was not the name of his horse.

THE FINANCIAL DISTRICT is built on a landfill covering the old ships of what was once Yerba Buena Cove.

UNION STREET, noted for its chic shops and restaurants, was called "Washerwoman's Lagoon," a valley once occupied almost exclusively by cows.

NOB HILL, was named after the English word "knob," meaning a rounded detached mountain or hill, or was it the British slang word for the rich? The Nevada silver kings and the railroad barons built flamboyant mansions on this hill, which they accessed by cable car.

IT'S ANYBODY'S GUESS how Russian Hill got its name. Legend has it that somewhere on this hill, Russian sailors were buried. Today it is a luxury residential district.

MORTON STREET, the infamous red-light district of the Barbary Coast, has been rechristened Maiden Lane. San Franciscans salute this exclusive shopping area with the annual Daffodil Festival.

ALAMO SQUARE INN

719 Scott Street
San Francisco, CA 94117
415-922-2055
Rooms $70–$225

THERE WAS A time in San Francisco when life was elegant... when people of vision built homes that became history. At Alamo Square Inn you relive that grand era in such a historic home—an immaculately restored Victorian mansion. You are afforded continental style accommodations, spectacular city panoramas, quiet walks in the private garden or in Alamo Square.

The accommodations include 15 rooms and suites, with freshly cut flowers from the garden accenting the opulent blend of Victorian and Oriental styles. The inn is finely appointed with European furnishings and Oriental rugs. Rich oak floors and warm wood paneling are complemented by an exquisite staircase illuminated by the stained glass skylight.

A full breakfast will be delivered in the privacy of your room or may be enjoyed in the garden or sun room. Complimentary late afternoon tea and wine are included in your room rate as well.

Prune Streusel

Preparation Time: One hour
Serves: 8
Pre-heat oven to 350°

2 cups all-purpose flour
½ tsp. baking powder
½ cup sugar
1 egg
5 oz. butter, cold and sliced
1 Tbsp. cinnamon
1 lb. prunes, halved, pitted and scored

Sift 1 cup flour and baking powder onto a baking board or marble counter. Push the center down to make an indentation. Add ¼ cup sugar and egg into center, working egg, sugar and flour together until soft. Add 2 oz. of butter and knead all ingredients into a soft ball.

Roll dough to ⅛ inch thickness and place in a buttered 11-inch springform baking pan. Poke several holes in base of dough and bake for 10 minutes until golden brown.

Prepare the streusel by combining 1 cup flour, ¼ cup sugar and 3 oz. butter with cinnamon. Place all the ingredients in a bowl and work together until crumbly.

Place the prunes into the pre-baked shell and sprinkle with streusel. Bake in the upper rack of the oven for 20 to 30 minutes or until streusel takes on a light color.

Cooking tip: The streusel is best served after standing 12 to 24 hours so as to allow moisture from the prunes to be fully absorbed into the crust.

THE ARCHBISHOPS MANSION INN

1000 Fulton Street
San Francisco, CA 94117
415-563-7872
Rooms $100–$265

THE ARCHBISHOP OF San Francisco, for whom this mansion was built in 1904, would be pleasantly surprised that it is now an elegant and delightfully romantic bed and breakfast inn. Every guest room is custom-designed to create an atmosphere reminiscent of the last century.

Amenities include exquisite antiques, embroidered linens, and comfortable sitting areas. Most rooms have fireplaces. All the comforts of home are at hand; lovely private baths, stacks of towels, French-milled soaps, and private phones.

Because the Opera House is a short six blocks away, the mansion's elegant 15 guest rooms are all named for operas. The inn is centrally located on a beautiful park surrounded by loved and much-photo-graphed Victorian homes.

Pampering is the rule here with breakfast served bedside in French picnic baskets and complimentary wine in the parlor—all included in your room rate.

Heavenly Chicken Liver Pate with Port and Currants

Preparation Time: 25 Minutes
Serves: 10

1½ cup port
  1 lb. chicken livers
  1 large yellow onion, chopped
  1 large garlic clove, chopped
½ cup currants
  1 tsp. Italian seasoning
¼ lb. salted butter, sliced
  Dash of cayenne

Warm the port in a small pot but do not boil. Add the currants and set aside.

Sauté the onions in a large skillet until they are a rich caramelized brown. Add the chicken livers and garlic, stirring until the outside of the chicken is brown and the inside is still pink. Add the port, currants, Italian seasoning and cayenne and reduce to a simmer, stirring for 1 minute. Remove from heat and cool.

Put the chicken mixture into a blender with the butter at a high speed until the pâté is smooth and pudding-like.

Spoon into a small serving bowl and cover with plastic wrap. Chill until firm.

Cooking tip: Serve with French bread or unsalted crackers and a chilled crisp Fumé Blanc.

Campton Place Hotel

CAMPTON PLACE RESTAURANT
340 Stockton Street
San Francisco, CA 94108
415-781-5555
800-235-4300 CA
800-647-4007 USA
Rooms $200—$850

THIS LUXURY HOTEL in the European tradition opened in 1983 after a massive $18-million renovation. Part of the character of Campton Place comes from its origins; two turn-of-the-century buildings gutted, rebuilt and transformed to accommodate 126 gracious rooms and suites, half a block from Union Square.

Guestrooms have a relaxing residential character. Furnishings include oversize beds with comforters, Henredon armoires housing color television with remote control panel by the bedside, Louis XVI writing desks and limited edition art by contemporary artists.

Amenities and services include a choice of five complimentary newspapers delivered daily, 24-hour concierge and valet services, 24-hour room service, valet parking, traditional evening turndown and daily in-house laundry and dry cleaning.

Pickled Salmon on Rye Toast with Dill Aioli

Preparation Time: 30 Minutes

Croutons:
- ¼ lb. butter
- 1 clove garlic, smashed
- ¼ rye baguette

Aioli:
- ½ tsp. garlic, chopped
- 1 Tbsp. fresh dill, chopped
- 2 Tbsps. lemon juice
- 2–3 Tbsps. warm water
- Cayenne
- Salt and pepper to taste
- 1 cup olive oil

Salmon Pickling:
- 8 cloves garlic, smashed
- 10 allspice berries, smashed
- 4 Tbsps. sugar
- 2 Tbsps. salt
- 2 Tbsps. black pepper corns
- 1 pint water
- 1 cup champagne vinegar
- ¼ cup lemon juice
- 8–10 oz. salmon, cut into 1½ oz. squares
- 1 large yellow onion, sliced
- Dill Garnish

To make croutons, in a small pan melt butter with garlic. Slice baguette into ¼" croutons. Butter both sides with garlic butter. Toast croutons and set aside.

To make aioli, in a food processor combine the first six ingredients. Run processor for 1 minute. Slowly add the olive oil to make a mayonnaise texture.

The salmon pickling procedure can be done 1 day in advance. In a cheesecloth sachet, tie the garlic, allspice berries, sugar, salt and pepper corns. Bring the water, vinegar, lemon juice and sachet to a boil. Cover pan and simmer for 5 minutes.

Place salmon and onions in stainless steel bowl. Pour hot liquid over fish and onions. Cover and refrigerate.

Spoon the aioli onto croutons, top with onion and salmon. Garnish with sprig of dill.

FOUR SEASONS CLIFT HOTEL

495 Geary Street
San Francisco, CA 94102
415-775-4700
800-332-3442
Rooms $180–$245

SERVICE. THAT'S WHAT the Four Seasons Clift is all about. Want champagne and caviar for breakfast? A $4,000 Galanos ballgown pressed at 3 a.m.? Or, like a recent winter visitor, four pack of BVD's, a whole uncut watermelon and 12 peaches within an hour? Consider it done. A guest never has to wait in the lobby, for instance. The Lobby Squad, made up of top management staff, patrols the check-in area to ensure rapid registration and a personal escort to the guest quarters.

Upstairs, sweeping draperies, original artworks and furnishings in the Georgian style welcome guests to voluminous private spaces filled with natural light. In a restful color scheme of gray-blue and dusky-rose, Clift dwellers enjoy details like clip-on reading lights, French bubble bath and plush terry robes.

You may not be a star, but after a stay at the fabulous Clift, you'll feel like one.

Dolmas

Preparation Time: 2 Hours
Pre-heat oven to 300°

  ½ **cup white rice, cooked**
  ½ **cup wild rice, cooked**
  ½ **lb. ground lamb**
  2 **Tbsps. fresh thyme, chopped**
  2 **Tbsps. fresh rosemary, chopped**
  2 **Tbsps. fresh parsley, chopped**
  2 **Tbsps. fresh oregano, chopped**
  2 **Tbsps. garlic, chopped**
    Salt and pepper to taste
3½ **cups chicken stock**
    Juice of 2 lemons
24 **grape leaves**
 1 **cup olive oil**

In a large bowl, mix the rice, lamb, herbs, garlic, salt and pepper. Add ½ cup chicken stock and the juice of 1 lemon to the stuffing mixture.

Place 1 Tbsp. of filling at the bottom of each grape leaf and roll up, tucking in the ends of the grape leaf. Place the dolmas in a baking pan and add the remaining chicken stock, lemon juice and olive oil to cover.

Bake at 300° for 1½ hours, until the leaves are tender.

Cool and serve at room temperature.

INN AT THE OPERA

ACT IV RESTAURANT
333 Fulton Street
San Francisco, CA 94102
415-863-8400
800-423-9610 CA
800-325-2708 USA
Rooms $125–$220

IN A CITY of great hotels, there is one whose heritage and purpose are unique. Inn at the Opera was built more than a half century ago to cater to visiting opera stars performing in San Francisco's opera.

This elegant, 48-room luxury hotel serves a special kind of guest who seeks comfort and style in a home away from home.

Each guest room is done in soft pastels and filled with custom-made furnishings. Queen beds are lavishly covered with oversized pillows. Microwave ovens to warm snacks, and minibars stocked with such delicacies as pate, Brie, splits of champagne and California wines are provided in each room. European armoires house televisions and plush robes hang in the closets for your use. Bedside chocolates, turndown service and complimentary morning paper are also provided.

You need only luxuriate in comfort. The Inn takes care of the rest.

Sweet Anise Cornbread

Preparation Time: 35 Minutes
Yield: One loaf
Pre-heat oven to 375°

1½ cup cornmeal
  2 tsp. baking soda
  ¼ cup sugar
  ½ cup flour
  2 Tbsps. ground anise
  2 whole eggs and 1 yolk
  2 cups sour cream
  ⅓ cup butter, melted
  1 Tbsp. tomato paste

Mix the cornmeal, baking soda, sugar, flour and anise together with a wire whisk.

In a separate bowl combine the eggs, sour cream, butter and tomato paste.

Combine the wet and dry ingredients together until thoroughly mixed. Pour into a 9 × 12″ greased cake pan and bake for 20 minutes.

Serve with butter.

THE INN SAN FRANCISCO

943 South Van Ness Avenue
San Francisco, CA 94110
415-641-0188
Rooms $68–$160

ORIGINALLY BUILT ON Mansion Row in the early 1870's, this historic 27 room Italianate Victorian was the home of John English, his wife, and their seven children. A San Francisco City Commissioner, English, dubbed "The Potato King" for his vast holding in potato commodities, also raised champion race horses on the surrounding grounds.

Today The Inn has been lovingly and thoughtfully restored to create an inviting ambience of past splendor and elegance. Classical music, candlelight, and the fragrance of roses set a mood that take you back in time. A time enhanced by ornate woodwork, Oriental carpets, and marble fireplaces.

The 15 guest rooms are individually decorated with antique furnishings, fresh flowers, marble sinks and polished brass fixtures.

In the grand double parlors, amidst the sparkle of stained and bevelled glass, you will be treated to a generous breakfast buffet which is included in your room rate. On warm sunny days the flower-filled garden beckons you to eat in the shade of an old fig tree.

Apple Nut Bread

Preparation Time: 1 Hour
Yield: 3 Loaves

3 eggs
2 cups sugar
1¼ cups oil
1 tsp. vanilla
3 cups apples, chopped
3 cups flour
1 tsp. salt
1 tsp. soda
1 cup nuts, chopped

Mix the eggs, sugar, oil and vanilla in a large bowl, until blended. Add the apples and set aside.

Sift together the flour, salt and soda.

Add the apple batter to the flour. Stir in the nuts and blend well.

Bake in 3 greased loaf pans. Start with a cold oven. Set at 325° and bake for 45 minutes. Check for doneness by inserting a knife in the middle of the loaf. If it comes out clean, it is done.

THE MAJESTIC

CAFE MAJESTIC
1500 Sutter Street
San Francisco, CA 94109
415-441-1100
800-869-8966 USA
Rooms $95–$200

ORIGINALLY BUILT IN 1902, the Majestic was one of San Francisco's earliest grand hotels. Restored beyond its initial elegance and grandeur, The Majestic has been honored with the prestigious Certificate of Recognition for Architectural Preservation and Restoration by the California Heritage Council.

Sixty bedrooms, including nine luxurious suites, are individually designed with a unique blend of French Empire and English antiques, custom furniture and soft-hued fabrics to elicit memories of a genteel and elegant home. The focal point of each room is a large, hand-painted, four-poster canopied bed laden with soft tapestries, feather pillows, comforters and fine linens. Most rooms are further enhanced by a warm glow from the fireplace and a romantic view of San Francisco.

Quiet, impeccable, old world manners reign in this magnificent five-story Edwardian structure, along with a warm hospitality normally reserved for long-cherished friends. Guests of The Majestic are welcomed more as house guests than as hotel residents.

Rainbow Vegetable Terrine

Preparation Time: 2 Hours
Serves: 15
Pre-heat oven to 350°

  2 cups carrots, cooked
  2 cups parsnips, cooked
  2 cups red beets, cooked
  2 cups broccoli, cooked
 11 eggs
  1 tsp. salt
  1 tsp. white pepper
  2 cups heavy cream
    Pinch nutmeg
    Pinch cumin

In a food processor, combine together carrots, ¼ cup cream, 3 eggs and pinch of salt and pepper. Puree and set aside.

Next, combine in a food processor, parsnips, 3 eggs, ¼ cup cream, pinch of cumin, and pinch of salt and pepper. Puree and set aside.

Combine red beets in food processor with 3 eggs, ¼ cup cream and pinch of salt and pepper. Puree and set aside.

Combine broccoli, 2 eggs, ¼ cup cream, pinch of nutmeg and pinch of salt and pepper. Puree and set aside.

In a buttered loaf pan, layer the vegetable purees carefully, one upon another until the pan is filled to the top. Sequence is important: bottom to top—carrot, beet, parsnip and broccoli.

Cover with parchment paper and place in a covered bain marie, so that the loaf pan cooks in the pan of water. Bake in a 350° oven for 1½ hours.

PETITE AUBERGE

863 Bush Street
San Francisco, CA 94108
415-928-6000
Rooms $105–$155

UPON ENTERING PETITE Auberge, you are transported immediately into the romantic comfort of a French country inn. An antique carousel horse, burnished woods and fresh cut flowers offer a warm reception.

Each of the 26 rooms is decorated with antiques and reproduction furniture, soft colored wallpapers, quilted spreads, handmade pillows, fresh flowers and fruit to reflect the French country mood. Most rooms have fireplaces. Evening turn down service and morning newspapers are provided.

The guest lounge and dining room are located downstairs and look out onto a side garden. Guests help themselves to a full breakfast of homemade breads and pastries, a hot dish, fresh seasonal fruit platters, juices and select coffees and teas, which are all included in the room rate.

Smoked Salmon Cheesecake

Preparation Time: 1½ Hours
Serves: 14
Pre-heat oven to 325°

1½ Tbsps. butter
 ½ cup bread crumbs, toasted
 ¾ cup gruyere cheese
 1 Tbsp. fresh dill
1¾ lb. cream cheese, room temperature
 4 eggs
 ⅓ cup half and half
 1 onion, sautéed
 ½ lb. smoked salmon, flaked

Butter a 9″ springform pan. Mix the bread crumbs, ¼ cup cheese and dill. Sprinkle the mixture into the pan, turning to coat. Refrigerate while preparing the filling.

Combine the cream cheese and eggs in a food processor or blender. Add the half and half. Fold in the cheese, onion and salmon.

Pour the mixture into the springform pan and place in a larger roasting pan. Add hot water to the halfway point of the springform pan.

Bake at 325° for 1 hour and 20 minutes. Turn off the oven and cool the cheesecake about one hour in oven with door ajar. Transfer to cooling rack. Cool to room temperature before removing from pan.

Sour Cream Coffeecake

Preparation Time: 1½ Hours
Pre-heat oven to 350°
Yield: 1 bundt pan—10"

  1 cup butter, softened (2 sticks)
2¾ cups sugar
  2 eggs, beaten
  2 cups sour cream
  1 Tbsp. vanilla
  2 cups white flour
  1 Tbsp. baking powder
  ⅛ tsp. salt
  2 cups pecans, chopped
  2 Tbsps. cinnamon

Grease and flour bundt pan.

Cream the butter and 2 cups of the sugar. Add eggs and blend. Add the sour cream and vanilla.

Sift together the flour, baking powder and salt. Fold the dry ingredients into the creamed mixture, and beat until just blended. Do not overbeat.

Mix together remaining ¾ cups sugar with pecans and cinnamon.

Pour half of the batter into the bundt pan. Sprinkle with half the pecan and sugar mixture. Add the remaining batter and top with the remaining pecan mixture.

Bake at 350° for 1 hour. Serve warm.

Spinach and Feta Cheese Triangles

Preparation Time: 45 Minutes (note refrigeration time)
Pre-heat oven to 400°
Yields: 35–40

  4 Tbsps. oil
  3 onions, finely chopped
24 oz. spinach, fresh or frozen
  2 Tbsps. dill
  8 oz. feta cheese, crumbled
  2 eggs, beaten
  6 Tbsps. sour cream
    Dash of nutmeg
    Salt and pepper
    Puff pastry

Sauté the onions in oil until tender. Stir in the spinach. Cook 5 minutes longer. Stir in the dill and cheese. Cool. Mix in the eggs, sour cream, nutmeg and season with salt and pepper. Refrigerate until cold.

Cut the puff pastry into 4″ squares and place on a sheet pan. In the center of each pastry, place 1 Tbsp. of filling. Fold the opposite corners over to form a triangle. Press the edges together with a fork to seal.

Bake at 400° for 15–20 minutes.

THE QUEEN ANNE HOTEL

1590 Sutter Street at Octavia
San Francisco, CA 94109
415-441-2828
800-262-2663 CA
800-227-3970 USA
Rooms $94–$125

THIS GRAND QUEEN ANNE style Victorian was originally Miss Mary Lake's School for girls in 1890, which offered upper class young women an opportunity to groom themselves for their future roles in San Francisco society.

Throughout The Queen Anne, care was taken to preserve its rich history. Each of the 49 guest rooms is individually decorated with English and American antiques.

Guests enjoy a complimentary continental breakfast served in their rooms each morning along with the morning paper, or in the beautiful mahogany wainscoted parlor. The library is the ideal setting for the partaking of afternoon refreshments provided for all guests.

Smoked Salmon Pasta

Preparation Time: 20 Minutes
Serves: 6

5 Tbsp. butter
3 shallots, minced
3 cloves garlic, minced
1½ cups whipping cream
2 Tbsps. vodka
¼ tsp. ground white pepper
4½ oz. smoked salmon, diced
1½ lbs. fresh fettuccine
3 oz. salmon caviar, optional
3 Tbsps. chives, minced, optional

In a large skillet over medium heat, melt butter and sauté the shallots and garlic for 2 minutes. Pour in the cream and stir, while bringing to a boil. Lower the heat and simmer until the cream has reduced slightly, about 10 minutes. Stir in the vodka, white pepper and smoked salmon. Heat thoroughly. Remove from heat.

Cook pasta in boiling water until slightly chewy (al dente) about 30 seconds. Drain the pasta. Add the cooked pasta to the sauce.

Serve on warmed plates, sprinkled with salmon caviar and chives.

*Reprinted by permission of Ortho Information Services.

THE SHERMAN HOUSE

2160 Green Street
San Francisco, CA 94123
415-563-3600
Rooms $210–$700

THIS INTIMATE GRAND hotel boasts heritage, luxury and elegance. The gleaming white Italianate Victorian 15-room hotel with the mansard roof sits quietly on a residential street in the Pacific Heights district, overlooking the Bay.

The large west wing consists of a three-story music and reception room, enlivened by an ornate, leaded-glass skylight. The main floor of the east wing includes a large sitting room with a double mahogany staircase leading down to the music room, a solarium and a long, rectangular dining room, whose windows overlook the gardens. The house includes magnificently refinished hardwood floors and 14 wood-burning fireplaces with marble mantelpieces.

All the guest rooms have queen-sized heavily draped canopy beds with imported down comforters. The sound system is hidden in the fabric-covered walls. Each of the elegant, black granite bathrooms has a miniature television set and a second telephone.

In back of the house is a third-of-an-acre of formal, private gardens. The walkways have been repaved with cobblestones obtained from the Cable Car Restoration Project.

THE SHERMAN HOUSE

Brioche French Toast Stuffed with Apples & Honey Cider Sauce

Preparation Time: 30 Minutes
Serves 4

2 cups apples, diced
1 tsp. sugar
4 brioches, sliced thick
4 eggs
1 cup cream
1 tsp. cinnamon
1 cup walnuts, toasted
1 cup apple cider
1 cup honey
2 oz. butter

Sauté apples in butter until golden. Stir in sugar and let caramelize. Remove from heat and cool.

Make a small incision on the side of each slice of brioche and stuff with apples, using a small spoon. Press gently to seal the bread.

Whip eggs, cream and cinnamon together. Dip each slice into the egg mixture and brown each side on the griddle. Keep warm in the oven while you make the sauce.

Bring the cider and honey to a boil. Remove from heat and whisk in butter.

Place brioche on heated plates. Sprinkle with walnuts and pour the sauce over the brioche.

SPENCER HOUSE

1080 Haight Street
San Francisco, CA 94117
415-626-9205
Rooms $95–$155

THIS VICTORIAN QUEEN ANNE-style landmark offers the elegance of a luxury inn with all the comforts of a private home. Oversized plush sofas and deep chairs invite guests to nestle in plump cushions. Under the big bay windows, Oriental rugs are scattered on hardwood floors. The ambiance is private and romantic.

Each of the 6 bedrooms boasts heirloom furnishings, antique linens, down quilts and feather mattresses. Imported fabrics from England enhance windows that are fitted with hand-blown glass panes.

A delicious complimentary full breakfast is served fireside, in the formal dining room. Linen-topped tables are formally set with china and silver, but guests are made to feel quite at home as they wander to the kitchen for a chat and a cup of coffee with the innkeepers.

Pecan Orange Yeasted Waffles

Preparation Time: 15 Minutes (note refrigeration time)
Serves 8

½ cup warm water
1 package dry yeast
1 tsp. sugar
2 cups milk, warmed
½ cup butter, melted
1 tsp. salt
2¼ cups flour
2 eggs
¼ tsp. baking soda
⅓ cup pecans or walnuts, finely chopped
   Grated rind of one orange

Place the water in a large bowl and sprinkle in the yeast and sugar until it has dissolved, approximately 5 to 10 minutes.

Add the milk, butter, salt and flour and beat until smooth. Cover the bowl with plastic and let stand overnight at room temperature.

Before cooking waffles, beat in eggs and baking soda, pecans or walnuts and the grated orange. The batter will be thin.

Bake in a hot waffle iron.

Cooking tip: The batter will keep 4 or 5 days in the refrigerator.

Raspberry Coconut Coffee Cake

Preparation Time: 1½ Hours
Serves 12
Pre-heat oven to 350°

2¼ cups flour
  1 cup sugar
  ¾ cup butter, sliced
  ½ tsp. baking powder
  ½ tsp. baking soda
  ¾ cup sour cream
  2 eggs
  2 tsps. almond extract
  8 oz. cream cheese, softened
  ½ cup raspberry preserves
  ½ cup almonds, sliced
  ½ cup coconut, shredded

Spray or oil bottom and sides of a 9″ or 10″ springform pan.

In a large bowl combine flour, ¾ cup sugar and butter until mixture resembles coarse crumbs. Reserve 1 cup of crumb mixture and set aside. To remaining crumb mixture add baking powder, baking soda, sour cream, 1 egg and 1 teaspoon of almond extract. Blend well. Spread the batter over the bottom and 2 inches up the sides of the prepared pan.

In a small bowl combine the cream cheese, ¼ cup sugar, 1 egg and 1 teaspoon almond extract, blending well. Pour the mixture over the batter in the pan. Spoon the preserves over the batter and the coconut over the preserves.

In a small bowl mix the sliced almonds with the 1 cup crumb mixture and sprinkle over the top of the coconut.

Bake at 350° for 50 minutes or until cheese filling is set and the crust is brown. Serve warm.

Mexican Eggs

Preparation Time: 15 Minutes
Serves 8
Pre-heat oven to 375°

16 eggs
¼ cup water
1 small can green chiles, diced
1 small bunch green onions, sliced
¾ cup grated cheese, jack or cheddar
1 cup salsa
1 cup sour cream
8 flour tortillas
  Salt and pepper to taste

Beat the eggs until blended. Add the water, green chiles and green onions. Mix well. Season with salt and pepper.

Scramble the eggs in a large frying pan on top of the stove until nearly done, approximately 5 to 7 minutes. Sprinkle with cheese and place the pan in a 375° oven for 5 minutes or until the cheese is melted.

Cut the eggs into wedges and top with salsa and a dollop of sour cream. Serve with warm flour tortillas that have been buttered.

VICTORIAN INN ON THE PARK

301 Lyon Street
San Francisco, CA 94117
415-931-1830
Rooms $81–$138

THE VICTORIAN INN on the Park, a registered historic land-mark, also known as the "Clunie House," was built in 1897. Its restoration seeks to retain and revive late 19th century elegance.

All of the 12 guest rooms are unique and each reflects Victorian San Francisco. Guest rooms include beautiful comforters, down pillows, fresh flowers and antique Queen Anne appointments that recreate turn of the century elegance.

Awake in the morning to French roasted coffee, homemade muffins and pumpkin date bread, which are served with freshly squeezed orange juice, a variety of fresh fruits and buttery croissants. Breakfast is included in your room rate.

The Inn is located across from Golden Gate Park in an area famed for its noble Victorians.

Blueberry Bread

Preparation Time: 1½ Hours
Yield: 2 Loaves
Pre-heat oven to 350°

   2 cups sugar
   3 cups flour
1½ tsps. soda
   1 tsp.salt
   2 tsps. cinnamon
   2 baskets of fresh blueberries
1¼ cup oil
   4 eggs, beaten

Grease and flour two bread pans 8" × 4".

Mix all dry ingredients in a large bowl, making a well in the center. Pour all liquid ingredients into the hole. Add the blueberries and mix by hand.

Bake at 350° for one hour or until done.

WESTIN ST. FRANCIS

335 Powell Street
San Francisco, CA 94102
415-397-7000
800-228-3000
Rooms $195–$400

THE WESTIN ST. FRANCIS, overlooking San Francisco's historic Union Square, has maintained its preeminence as the city's center of social, theatrical and business life since opening its doors in 1904. Today, its luster is as bright as ever, following the completion of a three-year, $32 million roof-to-sidewalk restoration program, and a recent $9 million renovation of the 32-story tower and 1,200 guest rooms.

Looking like exotic space capsules, the five outside elevators provide a vertical transportation system to move tower guests to their rooms at 1,000 feet per minute. The cars have bronze-tinted, laminated solar glass sides and offer a panoramic view of downtown San Francisco.

The great "Magneta" clock of carved rosewood in the main lobby was installed in 1906 as the master clock for all of the hotel clocks. It is San Francisco's most famous downtown rendezvous—"Meet me under the clock" means the St. Francis lobby.

Salted Cod Fish on Maui Onions

Preparation Time: 35 Minutes
Serves 4
Pre-heat oven to 350°

1½ lbs. small potatoes, roasted
2½ lbs. cod fish, salted
 2 oz. flour
 6 oz. olive oil
1½ lbs. Maui onions, sliced ⅛" thick
 2 branches parsley, chopped
 1 tsp. juniper berries
 One branch thyme
 2 bay leaves
 4 garlic cloves, crushed
 Salt and pepper to taste
 Lemon wedges for garnish

Roast potatoes until done. Set aside.

Desalt cod in fresh water and dry. Dust with flour and quickly fry in olive oil until golden brown.

In a baking-serving dish, layer the Maui onions with parsley, juniper berries, thyme, bay leaves and garlic. Arrange the sautéed fish and roasted potatoes on top. Season with salt and pepper.

Bake for 8 minutes at 350°. Serve in the baking dish with lemon wedges on the sides.

WHITE SWAN INN

845 Bush Street
San Francisco, CA 94108
415-775-1755
Rooms $145–$160

THE WHITE SWAN Inn is a six-story Nob Hill building with a marble facade, bay windows, and a rear deck. The Inn combines the elegant decor of an English garden inn with the sophistication of cosmopolitan San Francisco.

Heavy, beveled glass doors open to a large reception area with an antique carousel horse, antiques and English art. Downstairs is a private lobby for guests to enjoy complimentary afternoon tea and hors d'oeuvres in front of a welcome fire.

The English theme is well-reflected in the 26 guest rooms with warm polished woods, softly colored English wallpapers and prints, comfortable beds and separate sitting areas. Each room has a fireplace, fresh flowers and fruit, a wet bar and refrigerator.

Each morning a generous breakfast is served in the dining room just off the garden... warm homemade breads, pastries, cereal, fresh fruit and juices are tastefully presented. Breakfast and afternoon tea are included in your room rate.

Apple Walnut Sour Cream Bread

Preparation Time: 1½ Hours
Yield: 2 Loaves
Pre-heat oven to 350°

1 cup butter
1 cup brown sugar
4 eggs
2 tsps. vanilla
2 cups sour cream
2 cups flour
2 tsps. ground cardamon
2 tsps. baking soda
2 tsps. baking powder
½ tsp. salt
4 cups chopped apples
2 cups walnuts

Cream butter and sugar until fluffy. Add the eggs and vanilla. Beat until smooth. Add the sour cream. Set aside.

In a large bowl mix the dry ingredients together. Gently fold in the butter mixture. Add the apples and walnuts, being careful to avoid over-mixing.

Bake in a 350° oven for 1 hour 10 minutes or until bread is done. Allow to cool completely before slicing.

Herbed Roulade

Preparation Time: One Hour
Pre-heat oven to 350°

2 Tbsps. oil
2 eggs
1 cup milk
½ cup flour
2 tsps. fresh chives
2 tsps. fresh dill
1 Tbsp. fresh parsley, chopped

Brush an 11"x 17" jelly roll pan with oil.

Beat the eggs for 15 seconds until pale yellow. Add the milk in a slow stream. Add the flour and mix until smooth. Add the herbs. Let the mixture rest for 30 minutes, then pour into the jelly roll pan.

Bake for 12 minutes at 350°. Cool in the pan and loosen the bottom with a metal spatula.

Filling

2 onions, chopped
1½ lbs. mushrooms, sliced
Butter for sautéing
5–6 ripe avocados, chopped
½ lb. grated cheddar cheese

Sauté onions and mushrooms. Mix all ingredients together. Spread filling over the entire crepe and roll lengthwise.

Heat slightly when ready to slice.

Marinated Mushrooms

Preparation Time: 15 Minutes (note refrigeration time)
Yield: 6 cups

2 lbs. small fresh mushrooms
2 cups water
2 tsps. salt
1 cup white vinegar
1 bay leaf
2 thyme sprigs
2 garlic cloves
4 Tbsps. olive oil
½ medium red onion, sliced
   Zest of one lemon
2 Tbsps. parsley, finely chopped

Trim mushroom stems. Wipe clean with a damp cloth. Put mushrooms in a heatproof bowl.

In a saucepan, combine water, salt, vinegar, bay leaf, thyme, garlic and oil. Bring to a boil and pour over the mushrooms. Cool. Cover and refrigerate for 12 hours.

To serve, drain mushrooms and place in a serving bowl. Discard bay leaf, thyme and garlic. Mix in sliced onion. Add lemon zest and garnish with parsley.

HOW YOU CAN MEASURE UP...

LIQUID MEASURES

1 dash	6 drops
1 teaspoon (tsp.)	⅓ tablespoon
1 tablespoon (Tbsp.)	3 teaspoons
1 tablespoon	½ fluid ounce
1 fluid ounce	2 tablespoons
1 cup	½ pint
1 cup	16 tablespoons
1 cup	8 fluid ounces
1 pint	2 cups
1 pint	16 fluid ounces

DRY MEASURES

1 dash	less than ⅛ teaspoon
1 teaspoon	⅓ tablespoon
1 tablespoon	3 teaspoons
¼ cup	4 tablespoons
⅓ cup	5 tablespoons plus 1 teaspoon
½ cup	8 tablespoons
⅔ cup	10 tablespoons plus 2 teaspoons
¾ cup	12 tablespoons
1 cup	16 tablespoons

VEGETABLES AND FRUITS

Apple (1 medium)	1 cup chopped
Avocado (1 medium)	1 cup mashed
Broccoli (1 stalk)	2 cups florets
Cabbage (1 large)	10 cups, chopped
Carrot (1 medium)	½ cup, diced
Celery (3 stalks)	1 cup, diced
Eggplant (1 medium)	4 cups, cubed
Lemon (1 medium)	2 tablespoons juice
Onion (1 medium)	1 cup, diced
Orange (1 medium)	½ cup juice
Parsley (1 bunch)	3 cups, chopped
Spinach (fresh), 12 cups, loosely packed	1 cup cooked
Tomato (1 medium)	¾ cup, diced
Zucchini (1 medium)	2 cups, diced

INDEX

Appetizers:
Bresaola, 203
Brie in pastry, 144
Chèvre with sundried
  tomatoes, 173
Chicken pâté, port & currants, 251
Chicken, Japanese, 192
Chicken, Jerk drumettes, 93
Chicken, Tandoori, 157
Clams in black bean sauce, 233
Clams, steamed with saffron, 131
Cod on Maui onions, 277
Crab cakes, 218, 225
Crab meat, Hollandaise sauce, 195
Cucumber dip (caciki), 149
Custard, garlic, 37
Dolmas, 255
Duck filet, mustard sauce, 193
Eggplant & mozzarella, 162
Eggplant, chicken, 198
Eggrolls, cheese & jalapeño, 241
Empanadillas with rabbit, 134
Fattoush, 89
Five-spice duck breasts, 101
Fritters, corn & lobster, 44
Lobster in mango cups, 112
Lobster teriyaki, 194
Mushrooms with olive
  tapenade, 31
Mushrooms, black, oyster
  sauce, 111
Mushrooms, marinated, 281
Mussels, tomato saffron broth, 51
Peppers with three cheeses, 50
Pork & eggplant banderillas, 133
Prawns, vanilla, 115
Pumpkin & red pepper slippers, 67
Rabbit pastry, 118
Radicchio, grilled, 179
Radicchio, marinated, grilled, 161
Roulade, herbed, 280
Salmon, carpaccio, 217
Salmon, coriander, cured, 83
Salmon, corn pancake, 125
Salmon, pickled, dill aioli, 253
Salmon, smoked, asparagus, 191
Salmon, smoked, cheesecake, 263
Scallops, spicy, 38
Shrimp, feta, vinaigrette, 185
Shrimp, lime garlic, 95
Spanakopita, 150
Spinach & feta cheese triangles, 265
Squab, minced, 106
Sweet potato fries, 52
Tartare, Bix, 25
Trout, smoked, pâté, 87
Tuna ceviche, papaya, avocado, 211
Vegetable terrine, 261
Won ton with crab, 114

Breakfast, Breads & Muffins:
Biscuits, cardamon, 138
Bread, apple nut, 259
Bread, apple walnut sour
  cream, 279
Bread, blueberry, 275
Brioche French toast, 269
Coffeecake, raspberry coconut, 272
Coffeecake, sour cream, 264
Cornbread, sweet anise, 257
Eggs, Mexican, 273
Fattoush, 89
Streusel, prune, 249
Waffles, pecan orange, yeasted, 271

Condiments:
Five-spice powder, 90
Ginger, pickled, 102
Jam, red pepper, 230
Jelly, jalapeño, 52
Marmalade, sweet onion, 120
Mayonnaise, 219
Mustard, ginger, 117
Pesto, cilantro, 230
Remoulade, 226
Remoulade, celery root, 204
Sauce, dipping, 241

Desserts:
Anglaise, amaretto crème, 123
Bananas, glazed, 109
Beaujolais granite, 208
Berries, pannequet of, 65
Cake, flourless chocolate, 85
Cake, poppyseed, 41
Cake, sponge, 59
Chocolate with Amaretti
  cookies, 165

Cookies, black pepper butter, 209
Cookies, Turkish, 153
Crème anglaise, 231
Crème brûlée, 237
Crème brûlée, Bix, 29
Crème brûlée, carmelized
    apples, 129
Crème brûlée, mint & berries, 35
Custard, brown, 243
Flan, orange, 135
Fruits with calvados sabayon, 141
Ginger moons, spicy, 103
Ice cream, guava, 215
Mousse, chocolate & vanilla, 123
Pie, chocolate black walnut, 53
Pie, pumpkin, 215
Pone, sweet potato, 97
Pot de crème, caramel, 91
Pudding, rice (kheer), 159
Sauce, caramel, 91
Soufflé, macadamia nut, 47
Tart, Italian plum almond, 79
Tart, lemon, 147
Tart, raspberry walnut, 183
Tartlets, apple & blueberry, 231
Tiramisu, 189
Tiramisu, Majestic, 70
Torte, chocolate, 223

Fish and Shellfish:
Calamari & artichoke salad, 234
Clams, saffron & pinenuts, 131
Cod on Maui onions, 277
Crab cakes, 218, 225
Crab meat, Hollandaise sauce, 195
Crab salad, 62
Crab won ton, 114
Halibut encrusted with
    potatoes, 169
Lobster & corn fritters, 45
Lobster in mango cups, 112
Lobster teriyaki, 194
Lobster, sautérne ginger butter, 139
Mussel, soufflé, 220
Mussels, tomato saffron broth, 51
Paella, 242
Prawn soup, 240
Prawns with feta, 151
Prawns, cilantro pesto, 229

Prawns, vanilla, 115
Salmon, beurre blanc, 236
Salmon, carpaccio, 211
Salmon, coriander, cured, 83
Salmon, corn pancake, 125
Salmon, fennel vinaigrette, 145
Salmon, grilled, 228
Salmon, pickled, rye toast, 253
Salmon, smoked, asparagus, 191
Salmon, smoked, cheesecake, 263
Salmon, smoked, pasta, 267
Scallops, spicy, 38
Seafood sausage gumbo, 227
Seafood tempura, 200
Shrimp & feta cheese, 185
Shrimp salad, 94
Shrimp, lime garlic, 95
Sole, filet, 119
Trout, smoked, pâté, 87
Tuna ceviche, 211
Tuna with white beans, 186
Tuna, peppered, 207

Meat:
Bresaola, 203
Empanadillas, rabbit, olives, 134
Goat, curried, 96
Lamb loin en croute, 63
Lamb, Mongolian, 107
Lamb, roast leg of, 152
Lamb Shahi Korma, 156
Lamb shanks, 46, 63
Lamb stuffed with caponata, 170
Mignon, filet, 182
Pork & eggplant banderillas, 133
Rabbit pastry, 118
Rabbit with cabbage compote, 140
Rabbit with mustard, 146
Steak, skirt, 52
Sukiyaki, beef & vegetable, 201
Tartare, Bix, 25
Veal shanks in tomato sauce, 188
Venison, herbed, 213

Pasta:
Artichokes, spinach, pancetta,
    cream, 187
Mushroom fettuccine, 175
Pancetta, peas, cream, 163

Pesto, clams, white beans, 206
Pheasant ragout, 168
Salmon, smoked, 267

Poultry:
Chicken breasts stuffed, wine
   sauce, 164
Chicken curry pot pie, 40
Chicken eggplant, 198
Chicken hash, 27
Chicken in hazelnut sauce, 127
Chicken in Oriental five-spice, 90
Chicken liver pâté, 251
Chicken, grilled, 84
Chicken, Japanese style, 192
Chicken, Jerk drumettes, 93
Chicken, lemon grass, chile
   pepper, 113
Chicken, roasted pepper sauce, 176
Chicken, Tandoori, 157
Duck breasts, five-spice, 101
Duck filet with mustard sauce, 193
Guinea hen, roasted, 33
Pheasant ragout, 168
Squab, berry purée, 64
Squab, minced, 106
Turkey breast, 69

Salads and Dressings:
Artichokes, marinated, 132
Arugula, prosciutto, pear, 39
Baby lettuce, 49
Beet, bean, 167
Cabbage, duck fat, 56
Calamari, artichoke, 234
Coleslaw, 226
Crab, 62
Cucumber, 83
Dressing, Italian, 235
Dressing, lemon-miso, 82
Eggplant, arugula, 180
Goat cheese, ratatouille, 205
Greens, mixed, 82
Jicama, 239
Mayonnaise, 87
Pear, walnut, 73
Radishes, apples, oranges,
   cheese, 212
Red cabbage slaw, 99

Salade d'Avignon, 143
Scallop, prawn, 68
Shrimp & feta cheese, 185
Shrimp with tomatoes, 94
Trout, 215
Vegetables dressed with
   vinegar, 199
Vinaigrette, champagne, 49
Vinaigrette, citrus, 89
Vinaigrette, Dijon, 26
Vinaigrette, lime mint, 185
Vinaigrette, walnut sherry, 73
Vinaigrette, warm, 222
Waldorf with blue cheese, 26

Sauces:
Bix, 28
Black bean, 233
Black olive, 171
Calvados beurre blanc, 144
Cherry, 69
Dipping, 241
Garlic, 64
Hazelnut, 128
Honey mustard, 228
Lemon herb, 162
Mayonnaise, ancho, 38
Mushroom, 37
Mustard, 193
Nantua, 44
Oyster, 111
Pomegranate, 213
Port beurre rouge, 76
Salsa fresca, 50
Sautérne ginger butter, 139
Sukiyaki, 201
Vanilla, 115
Watercress, 126
Wine, 34

Soups:
Artichoke, 32
Avocado, 61
Butternut squash & leek, 74
Chicken, spinach, Caribbean, 43
Corn, cream of, 55
Hot & sour, 105
Lentil (dal), 155
Pea & lettuce, 88

Prawn, 240
Seafood sausage gumbo, 227
Soybean, 197
Squash & pear, 81
Squash, sweet mama, 100
Stock, 74
Stock, mushroom, 77
Tomato, sausage, foccacia, 174
Winter squash, cream of, 137

Vegetables and Side Dishes:
Beans, pinto, 46
Beets, mixed baby, 122
Cabbage compote, 140
Chanterelles, 121
Corn, sundried cherry, wild rice
   stuffing, 69
Eggplant & mozzarella, grilled, 162
Eggplant, chicken, 198

Eggplant, red-cooked, 108
Mushrooms, black, oyster
   sauce, 111
Mushrooms, marinated, 281
Polenta, 188
Polenta, rosemary, chanterelles, 34
Polenta, soft, 77
Radicchio, grilled, 161, 179
Ragout, vegetable, 78
Rice pillau, 158
Risotto bianco, 181
Risotto tambales, 171
Spanakopita, 150
Sweet potato fries, 52
Tamales, 214
Tempura, 200
Vegetable terrine, rainbow, 261
Vegetables, grilled, 75

ABOUT THE AUTHOR

KATHLEEN DEVANNA FISH, author of the popular "Secrets" series, is a gourmet cook who is always on the lookout for recipes with style and character.

In addition to "San Francisco's Cooking Secrets," the California native has written "Cape Cod's Cooking Secrets," "The Great California Cookbook," "California Wine Country Cooking Secrets," "Monterey's Cooking Secrets" and "Cooking and Traveling Inn Style."

Before embarking on a writing and publishing career, she owned and operated three businesses in the travel and hospitality industry.

She and her husband, Robert, and their black lab, Dreamer, live on a boat in the Monterey harbor.

ROBERT FISH, award-winning photojournalist, produces the images that bring together the concept of the "Secrets" series.

In addition to taking the cover photographs, Robert explores the food and wine of each region, helping to develop the overview upon which each book is based.

Bon Vivant Press
P.O. Box 1994
Monterey, CA 93942
800-524-6826   FAX 408-373-3567

Send _____ copies of "Cape Cod's Cooking Secrets"
at $14.95 each.

Send _____ copies of "The Great California Cookbook"
at $13.95 each.

Send _____ copies of "California Wine Country Cooking
Secrets of Napa/Sonoma" at $13.95 each.

Send _____ copies of "San Francisco's Cooking Secrets"
at $13.95 each.

Send _____ copies of "Monterey's Cooking Secrets"
at $13.95 each.

Add $3.00 postage and handling for the first book ordered and $1.50 for each additional book. Please add 7.25% sales tax for those books shipped to California addresses.

Please charge my □ Visa
□ MasterCard # _____

Expiration date _____ Signature _____

Enclosed is my check for _____

Name _____

Address _____

City _____ State _____ Zip _____

□ This is a gift. Send directly to:

Name _____

Address _____

City _____ State _____ Zip _____

□ Autographed by the author

Autographed to _____